The Kid Whisperer

Lorraine DiGesu Lamar
Faith, Hope, & Love Kids Ranch

By Ruth Bradford

TABLE OF CONTENTS

PROLOGUE

David and I took two of our children to visit the Faith Hope and Love Kids Ranch in the Philippines. Upon our return we challenged Ruth and Larry to step into this mission field and use their gifts of love and creativity to serve these very special little ones. This book is the outcome of their adventures among the spirited children of the Faith, Hope & Love Kids Ranch.

Cynthia Wester with Pastor David Wester of Calvary Chapel

ACKNOWLEGEMENTS

*1 Thessalonians 5:18 KJV In everything give thanks: for this
is the will of God in Christ Jesus concerning you.*

Without Lorraine and Celing Lamar, and their dedicated work with and for children of the Philippines, this book would not exist. Without the sacrificial giving of many people all over the world, FAITH, HOPE, & LOVE KIDS RANCH would not exist.

Thank you, Debby Emel, my daughter, for tireless editing.

I thank Larry, my husband from my youth, and partner in all our trips to the Philippines.

I give special thanks to Anna Rivera, my XLibris consultant.

May every word of this book bring glory to God our Father, because Jesus Christ is our Perfect Word.

It is our hope and prayer that everyone who reads this will not only be blessed, but gain wisdom in the care, training, and discipline of children everywhere.

Lorraine and her
mom, Kay DiGesu

Lorraine and Celing with their three
children: Micah, Catherine, and DJ.

FOREWORD

By Micah Lamar, Lorraine's middle son, written during
his last year of school on the ranch.

Miicah (left) and DJ are talented brothers and best friends.

THE IMPORTANCE OF BUILDING A STRONG FOUNDATION

I grew up in a Christian family and at an early age, I was taught that my attitude and character were extremely important. From what I've seen, good character and attitude do not come naturally. They have to be taught, and not only with words, but by example. In order to attain these qualities, a strong foundation must be built. Everyone knows that the deeper the foundation is, the stronger the building will be. The foundation of my life has been built with the fear of God, discipline, and lots of love.

The Bible says, 'Go and make disciples,' and it should start with your family. Discipline comes from the word disciple, and that's how my parents trained me. I was taught to have good manners, patience, respect, and many other character traits. I was taught to love God and also fear Him. All these characteristics were poured into my life for as long as I can remember. Having lots of rules has always been a part of my life. It's not always fun, but it's always good. I have had to wash dishes, wash laundry, and clean the house...not only just my room. And I have learned to do so much more! It was all part of a daily routine that my parents were consistent in enforcing. My parents had a goal and that was to 'train up a child in the way they should go and when they are old, they will not depart from it.' They did more than just tell me, they were my example in life and my goal is to one day be like them.

It's interesting how the ACE curriculum holds the same standards of how I was raised. I have been studying in the ACE curriculum since I was in kindergarten and my whole life until now. What I learned in school and at home was never a conflict, never a double-standard. I never struggled with all the rules in the PACES because I was used to rules. All the comic strips and wisdom principles made it fun to learn. And that's probably what I will never forget about the ACE. School was the longest part of my daily routine, and there were times when I got tired of working in PACE's but I had a goal, and that was to finish what I started.

Lorraine describes Micah this way: "Micah has always gotten along with his older brother and younger sister. He is what we call the 'peacemaker!' When we have problems at the ranch, Micah hates discord, and works to find solutions. He is focused and doesn't let anyone distract him...especially girls! Hehehe! Micah is sweet and thoughtful and there is no one else like him in the world...which, of course, is also true of every person I have ever met!"

DJ, Micah's older brother, and talented in the world of music, is amazed at how Micah gets the attention of so many kiddos to help them have fun at becoming physically fit.

PREFACE

"GO"

By Dave Lamar

"GO", is what most of us want to do. I believe the desire to go and change the world is embedded in all of us. We hear that small voice inside of us telling us to "GO" but for some reason we try to push that voice aside and pretend we didn't really hear it. We doubt the voice. We come up with all kinds of excuses: I'm not qualified, I'm not ready, I'm not healthy enough, or I'm not smart enough. And the list goes on.

The earliest memories I have as a kid are of our home of red cement floors and grey concrete walls. Our home was bare because a tile floor and painted walls were a luxury we could not afford yet. Chickens would nest on top of our walls and birds would fly in and out at will because we had no ceiling under the roof. Life was very simple, but it was the only life I knew, so it was good.

I knew I was different from the other children because I was the only white kid in school surrounded by brown-skinned Filipino kids. It must have been quite confusing seeing this white kid speaking fluent Tagalog.

Every day, Dad would pick me up from school and we would go straight to the government orphanage where my mom volunteered teaching the kids who lived there, how to read. The place smelled bad and the kids were always dirty. But all I knew, as a 7 year old, was that I wanted to play and those kids became my friends.

One Christmas, my mom convinced the people in our church to take some of the kids from the government orphanage home for the holidays. Mom helped place the kids with families, willing to share their home for a week or two. Mom explained that real Christmas JOY is: Jesus, Others, You. All the kids were chosen to go home with a family except two boys. The boy named Erwin had Down syndrome and the other boy was autistic. I hadn't noticed Erwin much at the orphanage before, but after Mom invited those two boys to our home for Christmas, I felt differently. We had so much fun, singing and laughing. Erwin had the sweetest spirit and was always smiling. He loved to dance and make everyone laugh. He had so much happiness and joy to share, despite his situation. Besides the Down syndrome, his eyes were crossed and he was pigeon toed. But I didn't see a boy with Down syndrome, I saw Erwin, just like any other kid who craved love and attention. He was just like me! I didn't know it as a seven year old, but that Christmas with Erwin was part of God's preparation for my life, which I never could have imagined.

Sometime later, I saw blueprints on our table. At first I heard my parents talking about helping the government orphanage more. But time went by and I heard my mom and dad saying, "What if we started our own orphanage?" That question was asked more and more often. Then one day Mom saw me looking at new blueprints of a huge two-story building.

She asked me, "What do you think? Do you think it will fit?"

I knew we didn't even have money to paint the walls of our own house, and we lived on a small property, so a big house and money for a bunch of kids seemed impossible.

Even though I was a kid with a wild imagination, I had my doubts. But the thought of having kids to laugh with, play with, and love all the time, excited me.

About a year later, the big building in the blueprint was built on our property. Then, we were on our way to meet one of the first boys to join our family. He was 6 years old, couldn't go to school because he took care of his invalid father, and his mother had died. His father sat on the floor on a little mat, and told us he couldn't care for his son any more. Tears streamed down his face, as he told us he wanted his son to go to school. He told his little boy that he wanted him to have a better life than what he could give him. He kissed his head and said goodbye.

On the way home, my brother, Micah, and my sister, Catherine, and I asked him questions and tried everything to get him to talk and laugh with us. Slowly, he began to smile and respond to us. We were so excited to have a new brother to play with!

Before long, our family of children had grown to over 30. With all the working, activities, fun, and games, we felt like we were at a youth camp every day. We ate together, studied together, played and did chores together. Several people who came to visit, often asked us if we ever got jealous because we didn't have the full attention of our parents. It seemed like a weird question for my brother and sister and me because we really enjoyed having all these children around calling our parents, "Mommy," and "Daddy." There was never a dull moment! We were having the time of our lives.

A story is never really complete without storms that threaten to destroy the ship of life you sail on. No matter how mighty and safe you think your ship is, the storms do come. After a few years of trial and error, getting the orphanage legal and licensed, the American who helped finance the orphanage and his friends formed a governing "Board." They decided that my parents weren't qualified to run the orphanage. They wanted a more "American" style of raising children. My parents' method of raising children was, and is, to prepare the children to become successful people in Filipino society. The "Board" gave my parents two choices: compromise or step down.

Stepping down was one of the most difficult things our family ever had to do. The "Board" wanted us to leave immediately after that decision. We were given one day to say our goodbyes to all the kids who had become our family. For nearly three years, we had worked, laughed, cried, and breathed the same air together every single day. Then, to be torn away from each other, was almost unbearable. We were never allowed to go back and see them again. In my 12-year old mind, I thought the "Board" people were heartless.

I had heard my mom tell people countless times about her dream of taking care of children like Mother Teresa. But then her dream fell apart. She felt like she had abandoned the very children she was committed to. But she knew that she could not compromise her God-given convictions of how to raise children. My mom's family encouraged her to return to New Mexico, but my dad's visa was denied, partly because of the aftermath of the tragedy that happened in the United States on September 11, 2001.

The first couple of weeks in the United States, we three kids had fun, because it was different. But then we got bored, and started fighting and misbehaving. After all, our lives had been filled with activity with almost 30 other kids every minute of every day.

Mom was sad. Dad wasn't with us. Mom would say things like, "What if we just stay here and send money to other missionaries?"

We three kids didn't want to stay in the United States. The Philippines was our home. We were miserable. We were bored. We told our mom, "We have to go back and start over!" Living a "normal life" for us was living with a bunch of kids! Otherwise, we were miserable.

Finally, after a very bad day, Mom told us that Dad was applying for a visa the third time. If he got it, he would come and we would really begin our life in New Mexico. We three kids started praying that Dad would not get it, so we could go home to the Philippines. That night Mom was waiting by the phone, to hear whether or not Dad got it and was buying a plane ticket.

When he called he said, "I GOT IT!...I got denied!" Mom was confused. Why did Dad get denied? But we knew God answered our prayers and we were the ones who would get plane tickets!

The "Board" bought the land from the first orphanage from Dad. That land was less than ½ an acre. But they paid Dad a good sum. He was able to buy 10 acres of land, and Mom and Dad planned the new orphanage. This time my parents were determined to trust only in God. Donations from many people were fine, but our family would not allow one important person to control the new orphanage.

We had not seen our dad for 6 months, so when we saw him at the airport, we were so excited! Mom and Dad asked us kids if we would be willing to help build the new orphanage. We all agreed that we would do everything we could do to help! From the airport, Dad took us straight to the new property.

"This is it! We're really gonn'a do this!" Dad was so enthusiastic.

It seemed like it was in the middle of nowhere. The weeds were thick and higher than our car. The only building on it was an old house on stilts. My dad and his brothers cleared the 10 acres with machetes, working 8 to 10 hours every day until it was clear. They cut down some of the coconut trees to reinforce the building so we could stay in it while the men cleared the land, which took a couple months. There was no electricity, so we rented a small apartment in town.

We needed money to put up the first building for the kids. Mom came up with the idea of selling t-shirts. Mom and some of her friends got together and decorated t-shirts with FAITH, HOPE, & LOVE Kids' Ranch using silk screens. They did hundreds of t-shirts. Mom didn't want to just take the shirts to the United States and beg for money or sell the shirts, so she came up with a plan. Mom found someone to teach Micah, Catherine and me several Filipino dances. We put together a little program with singing and dancing, using bamboo poles, coconut shells, and other props. We flew to the United States with 8 boxes of t-shirts. Dad still couldn't get a visa. Mom got us bookings at churches, prayer meetings, and other little gatherings many times each week, and sometimes twice in one day. We were on tour for three months. We would sing and dance, then Mom would share our visions and dreams about building an orphanage. She showed the t-shirts, but didn't put a price on them. She said that any donation was good to get a t-shirt. We ran out of t-shirts, but by then we had just enough money to start building the first house for the children. We flew home, and Dad and his brothers started construction.

Eventually, by word of mouth, news of Faith, Hope, & Love Kids' Ranch spread. Now, funds come in from all over the world, from people we don't even know.

God doesn't always call those who are qualified. God calls those who are willing. God doesn't care about your qualifications, or where you went to school, or what you've accomplished in your life. All God needs is a heart that is willing and patient in waiting. My mom was 18 years old when she moved to the Philippines. Faith, Hope, & Love Kids' Ranch is what it is today, because a young lady left the comforts of her own home at age 18 to serve God. She traveled to a country where she couldn't even speak the language. She married a Filipino man who also desired to serve God, but could hardly speak English. Together they have pursued their dreams of helping children and changing the world. My mom and dad have lived their lives in Faith, Hope, & Love, and continue to do so to this day.

All my life I have witnessed how God provides in the craziest of ways…especially when you think you're at the end of hope. My mom's favorite quote is, "Where God guides, He provides." And I'm a witness of that. God not only provides the food and clothing we need, but also the strength, wisdom, and people needed to keep us on our feet.

So don't ever let anyone tell you what you can or cannot do. As a 26 year old adult with my own dreams and goals, my life is built around the word, "GO"! If God tells you to do something, even if it scares you to death, just "GO"!

1   GOD'S CALL

O, God, thou art my God. Early will I seek thee: my soul thirsteth for thee;
my flesh longeth for thee in a dry and thirsty land. Psalm 63:1 KJV

Truly my soul waiteth upon God; from him cometh my salvation. Psalm 62:1KJV

What is it that drives a newly saved eighteen year old girl to return to the children of the Philippine Islands, especially after a disheartening mission trip? What is the deep driving desire that pushed Lorraine DiGesu into a lifelong commitment to helping abandoned, disadvantaged, abused, rejected children who knew no English, had no knowledge of the saving grace of Jesus, and were most likely to rebel against authority?

After seeing television commercials of Mother Teresa working with helpless children, young Lorraine DiGesu felt an overwhelming desire to serve the Lord Jesus in a foreign field. Lorraine thought she would go to India, but the Lord had a different plan. She came to the Philippines on a YWAM (Youth With A Mission) trip, right after she turned eighteen years old, right out of high school. She knew she wanted to serve the Lord, and fell head-over-heels in love with the children.

Not all missionaries in the field provide caring treatment for visiting teams, especially for teenagers. But we know our Lord can use good and bad experiences to impact our lives. Those missionaries in Lorraine's early life did not provide adequate drinking water, nor did they provide sufficient food, and the young people could not afford to buy good meals for themselves. Every one of the young people got dysentery or some other illness that ruined their desire to return to the Philippines. The Lord kept Lorraine safe from the physical attacks of the enemy, except for a few itchy parasites.

Lorraine commented on the whole experience, "It weeded out those people who just wanted a vacation from those who wanted to seriously serve the Lord!"

Lorraine DiGesu fell in deep, God-inspired love for the Filipino people, especially those who lived in poverty, and most especially the little children, who climbed in her lap and petted her hair and arms. They listened to her as she tried her best to communicate with them. The Holy Spirit had such a firm hold on Lorraine's heart strings that she knew she would return to the Philippines, no matter how hard family and friends tried to get her to stay home.

Lorraine has a special relationship with our Lord Jesus. He lives in and through her. He gives her wisdom in unique ways to solve tough problems with the children the Lord brings into her life. Lorraine thinks through, prays through, then quietly carries into action her God-given solutions and plans. Therefore the title of this book is: "The Kid Whisperer."

Not only does Lorraine have unique insight into overcoming behaviors, but also creative godly ways to solve problems. The Holy Spirit leads her to the right people and God leads the right people to her when she needs help for specific situations, quite often, even before the problems occur.

Lorraine explains it this way: "Our ideas and unique ways are designed to capture the child's attention and win their hearts with the love and joy of the Lord. Once we've done that, it's the feeling of leading them to find hidden treasure. These little people have so much to offer the world, but they're bound up in the pain of the mistakes of their parents. We need continued prayers for the kids and staff by all our supporters."

2 FAITH, HOPE, & LOVE KIDS RANCH

Deuteronomy 10:12-13 KJV Now…what doth the LORD thy God require
of thee, but to fear the Lord thy God, to walk in all His ways, to love Him,
and to serve the Lord thy God with all thy heart and with all thy soul,
to keep the commandments of the Lord… this day for thy good.

The road to serving God is not always what it seems. From the busy airport in Manila, the modern highways become smaller roads, and then a rutty jungle track closed in by palm trees, bushes and vines.

This is my favorite picture of Lorraine and me with the kids and their finished hand puppets.

Larry's and my jobs as short-term missionaries has been to help the kids in school and do special projects.

We brought paper towel tubes and solid fuel rocket engines. Larry helped the kids make rockets from scratch. Rocket day was exciting when the kids shot their individually painted rockets into the air. Some flew so high, they were out of sight. Most floated down successfully on their plastic bag parachutes, but a few came down outside FHL, much to the delight of the neighbors.

We learned so much more than we shared. Larry developed a few truisms after our first week, which evolved as we adjusted to life on the ranch:

1. Every day is a brand new bug that we've never seen before.

2. If it itches, it's just another bite; apply 'After Bite.'

3. If it feels like something is crawling on you; it is probably another bug.

4. 1st week: If there is a bug in your drink, dump it out. 3rd week: If there's a bug in your drink, pick it out. 5th week: If there's a bug in your drink, just go ahead and drink it! A little extra protein never hurt anybody!

5. If you look down and the floor looks like it's moving…it's time to sweep out the ants.

6. Don't try to pick up a spider with a tissue, it will immediately hop out of reach. A wiser choice is a broom!

Our first encounter with a truly BIG spider was about 2:00 in the morning. Ruth woke up and turned on the light. That particular spider, with the body type of a daddy-long-legs, and 8 spindly legs at least 12 inches long jumped across the wall. I awoke with a jerk to Ruth's squeals. I grabbed a broom, and like a true soldier, chased it and whacked at it all across the room. Finally, I made contact! Splat! Eight legs broke apart and scattered, still jerking with muscle spasms. I swept up the pieces and dumped them outside.

The next morning, Lorraine deflated my brave act by saying, "That spider is one our gentle giants. You should have just swept it…alive… outside the door!"

So much for heroism!'

3 PUT GOD FIRST

Matthew 22:37-39 KJV Jesus said unto him, "Thou shalt love the Lord thy God with all thy heart, and with all thy soul, and with all thy mind. This is the first and great commandment. And the second is like unto it, Thou shalt lovethy neighbor as thyself."

Routine is important for children to feel secure. Being consistent helps the children learn moment by moment what is expected and what they can and cannot do.

Monday through Friday the sound of a bike horn wakes the children up at 5:30 a.m. They must get ready for breakfast and for school, make their beds, and those who are cook's helpers must report to the kitchen. Before every meal they line up on sunny days outside the dining hall door. One of the kids reads a verse of the day and prays.

After breakfast, clean-up, and brushing teeth, the sound of a cow bell calls them to either the gym or back to the dining hall for morning devotions at 7:00. (Sometimes Mommy has just the younger children do morning devotions and she does evening devotions with the older children.) I had the privilege of doing the morning devotions two mornings a week, using puppet skits, flannel-graph Bible stories, and Gospel magic tricks, as well as teaching a few songs.

By 7:30 the children line up for school, all dressed in uniforms. The girls wear skirts and the boys wear long shorts. They all wear different colors of FHL shirts. On Mondays they salute the Bible, the Christian Flag, and the national Philippine flag. Next they sing the Philippine national anthem in Tagalog. The children remove their flip flops outside the door on the sidewalk and go into their classroom.

Fridays are special. The kids present Bible-based skits and sing and do choreography. The supervisors and monitors present awards and recognition for Paces finished. That first year, the three talented Lamar children lead Praise and Worship along with some of the older kids, playing the piano and drums. The children had been taught music by a young man for six weeks. But then he didn't work out, so from that time on, the older children taught the younger children to play instruments, dance, sing, and speak before an audience.

The children create their own dramas and dances using recorded Gospel songs. They also learn to play the drums, guitar, and keyboard. At times Lorraine has hired a music teacher but mostly they learn from one another.

Saturdays are designed for special cleaning, laundry, helping with whatever project Celing is working on, and special events. If the weather is good, the children who have earned privileges and have their school work caught up may get to take part in special things.

One favorite privilege is getting to walk to the bakery. Like most local Filipino bakeries, it is tucked into the jungle, reached by a dirt path. As we walk along, we pass pigs, vegetable gardens, water buffalo, and neighbors. Smoke from wood fires curls above the palm trees, and sweet yeasty smells draw us, before we actually get to the building. We walk around a large corrugated sheet of metal and we are inside the bakery.

Bakers are usually young men, who learn the trade from their fathers. The delicious concoctions are mixed and rolled out on long tables, cut into the desired shapes, laid out into pans and slid into the brick oven, heated by a wood fire on the side. One baker told me, with the help of one of the children who translated, that they must be careful how much wood they put into the fire box so as not to burn the product. The last step before putting the baked goods on delivery trucks is for a lady to wrap each item in plastic and seal it over an open flame.
The results are the most delicious, fresh, baked goods of chocolate, cinnamon, coconut, lemon and vanilla flavors, rivaling any in the world.

Sundays on the ranch are very special. The kids dress up in their very best clothes. All the laundry is off the lines. Occasionally, food packages of rice and other staples are prepared for families who come to church. Sunday school and church are the focus of the day. But it is also a day when families gather socially. The older children display their musical abilities by leading the time for Praise and Worship. Most songs are done in Tagalog. The church has grown from the ranch kids and a few staff members, to many families from the surrounding community. They have had as many as100 children in the Sunday School.

These girls are practicing for Sunday worship.
At times, the teams have performed in public schools. Sometimes as many as 600 students attend. Each time they are able to share the Gospel of Jesus.

4   CELISTINO (CELING) LAMAR

Larry and I were outside the dining hall and started talking to and asking Celing questions about his life. We talked and talked. One of the girls brought us bowls of popcorn and chairs. We continued talking until it got too dark for me to see my notes. What an amazing work, our Lord has done in the lives of Lorraine and Celing!

Celing was born into a fishing family on one of the smaller of the 7,107 islands and atolls (which are not always above water) of the Philippines. His family was very poor and if the fishing was poor, the children went hungry. Celing's only language was Tagalog, one of the main languages spoken by native Filipinos, later called Pilipino since the sound of 'f' is not in the native language. There are over 165 local dialects spoken in isolated villages. Many people never leave their village, so they live their whole life knowing little or nothing about the rest of the world. Cell phone and television reception is spotty in the outlying areas.

Celing is one of ten children. He has five brothers and four sisters. Celing and his siblings found plenty to do for fun when they were children. The ocean sand was their playground. Besides running and splashing, playing tag and ball, they learned to swim and fish like professionals.

One game they played involved a captured blow fish. They would squeeze the fish until it blew up. Then they played catch with the fish until the air came out its mouth and it died. Nature provides many such 'toys' for resourceful children.

Blue jelly fish were to be avoided because of their sting.

(As a side note, I, the author, experienced the instant pain of a direct encounter with the innocent-looking jellyfish! Three teen girls and I had just ridden bikes from the ranch three miles to Guis Guis Beach. I was teaching the girls to swim, when all of a sudden, I felt the sting of twenty tiny needle-like pricks! I had unknowingly encountered the tentacles of the blue jellyfish! About twenty minutes later, the ranch jeepney arrived with Lorraine and ten of the kiddos who had earned the privilege of a day at the beach. She saw my pale face and immediately asked the young lady, whose family owns that section of the beach, what to do. The lady smiled at the twenty red swelling dots on my foot. Then she stripped a handful of leaves from a vine and crushed them into a pulp in her hands. She carefully laid the green mass on the stings. Almost immediately, I felt relief.)

Celing laughed when he heard my story, indicating that jellyfish stings are commonplace. He added, "Jellyfish have no food value, but some of the men believe that if they have a hangover, they can boil the jellyfish and eat it. It will supposedly relieve the hangover." Celing made a face and laughed. "I never tried it!"

Celing went on with his story, "There was something within my heart that urged me to want more than a fisherman's existence. I didn't know it then, but the Holy Spirit was drawing me into a personal relationship with Jesus."

"Most Filipinos are 'religious.' My father, like many others had an altar in our home. My father's altar was elaborate with a very large Bible and candles that he kept lit. My father gave us kids strict instructions, 'Do not touch that Bible, or something bad will happen to you!' Those words, plus the Holy Spirit made me curious about that altar. My curiosity led me to look behind the curtain at the back of the altar. There I saw a small black Bible written in Tagalog. I took the little Bible."

"All of us kids had gone to a small school in our village, so we could read Tagalog. I took that little Bible and started to read. I wondered…there must be more! I couldn't really understand the stories, because it was before I received the Holy Spirit. But the words in that little Bible drew me in…I wasn't sure into what…yet. I knew I didn't want to be a fisherman. And I didn't want to be a Catholic priest. But I did know I wanted to serve God!"

"When I was sixteen, I finished school. The military wouldn't take me because I got migraine headaches. I went to Manila to go to school. I moved in with my sister and her husband, who lived above their bakery in Manila. I continued reading that Bible and knew I needed something more. I tried different churches, seeking the truth. I went to a Jehovah's Witness church, but when I tried to follow their teachings in my Bible, too many things did not agree. They wanted me to join their church and get involved, passing out their literature."

"I knew from reading and rereading the New Testament that the church started by Jesus Christ was just people…people who believed in Him. I went to a Baptist Church in Manila. It was there, I realized I was a sinner. I asked God to forgive me. The Holy Spirit was giving me understanding. But it bothered me that the Baptist Church also wanted me to join."

"I know the Holy Spirit continued to draw me into a serious relationship with Jesus Christ. After I met Lorraine and began going to church with her, I finally accepted Jesus as my Savior. Then the Holy Spirit opened up more and more a deeper understanding of God's Word. God answered my three questions about who God is, what is the right religion, and the real way to salvation."

"After we married, spent time in America, then returned to the Philippines, I knew the Holy Spirit wanted me to teach others what God had been teaching me. The new orphanage was going well. We hired a cook, caregivers, teachers, and men to help with the cows, building, and the grounds. I started teaching morning devotions to staff members. We made devotions a part of their work day."   Celing has asked different pastors to help him along his path to becoming a pastor. One such pastor is Pastor Oscar. He and his wife, Bobette, drive from Manila every other Sunday to preach. Pastor Oscar is a gifted Filipino preacher, whose humor and compassion are very much like Celing's. Their style of teaching God's Word is to focus on a Bible passage, then use humor and personal testimony stories. They each make their points clear and encourage the people to read along from the Bible. They make sure each person has a Bible.

Pastor Oscar and Celing make a wonderful preaching team. When we first started FHL, the congregation consisted of the kids and staff. Now it has grown to 50 to 60 adults and children from the community. On special Sundays, there may be as many as 100 children in the Sunday school. The community gathers to hear the Word of God in Tagalog. Their teaching is sincere and applies to the hearts of the people. Many people have come to know Jesus as their personal Savior because of their obedience to the leading of the Holy Spirit. When there are English speaking visitors like us, they translate their main points into English. But often we have to ask afterwards to explain their jokes!

5 LORRAINE AND CELING

Lorraine had come back to Manila in the Philippines, on her own. The Holy Spirit drew her, even though she had originally wanted to go to college and become an elementary school teacher, Lorraine knew without a shadow of a doubt, that God was calling her back to the Philippines to be a full time missionary. She said, " I stayed with a woman in a squatters' village, when I first came."

Thousands of Filipino families live far below poverty level. One person in a large extended family may work. The money they bring home is used for food. Squatter houses sprout up overnight on land owned by someone else. Dwellings are put together from whatever materials can be scrounged. Lack of proper plumbing or garbage disposal creates unhealthy living conditions and over-powering odors.

Lorraine added, "I was working in a private school, but they fired me when I refused to lay hands on children to 'slay them in the spirit.' Celing's sister invited me to live with her and her husband above their bakery. They had several rooms. Celing and the other bakers lived in one room, and I stayed in another room."

Celing is just over five feet tall with broad shoulders. He has dark wavy hair with a touch of gray and expressive brown eyes. When he smiles, his even white teeth show, and wrinkles appear at the corners of his eyes. His whole being expresses joy, which comes from a lifetime of walking with the Lord. When he teases or jokes, his eyebrows waggle. His nose is small, typical of the carefully sculpted Filipino features. Celing's skin is an even tan, the color of maple syrup. He almost always wears shorts, a tee-shirt and sandals or flip-flops.

Celing continued, "I was staying with my sister and her family above the bakery. I got up early to bake, then my brother-in-law delivered sandwich-style bread to the Filipino Army and Air Force bases. When they were on high alert, they could not accept deliveries, so we ground the left-over bread to be used as fillers in other baked goods."

"I took courses in air conditioning and refrigeration. I was learning airplane mechanics, too."

Lorraine smiled when she described her life living above the bakery. "I first really noticed Celing when we happened to be washing clothes at the pump at the same time each day. At first we didn't say anything, just smiled. I was still learning Tagalog and Celing didn't speak much English and was very shy. Then we started talking a little until my Tagalog ran out and his English ran out. I had noticed him reading his Bible. One day I invited him to the church I was going to. About the third time the pastor gave the invitation for salvation, Celing went forward."

Celing continued, "I received the Holy Spirit. Then I really began to understand the Bible. By then, Lorraine and I knew we wanted to get married. Lorraine wanted to have our wedding in my village. Her mom and dad, Kay and Mario, and all her family came to the Philippines."

Kay DiGesu, Lorraine's mom, remembers the day well. "I was worried about going across the ocean in such a small fishing boat to Celing's home island. We had everything for the wedding in those small boats. But it was okay. God kept us safe, just like the fishermen on Lake Galilee were kept safe in the storm because Jesus was with them. Jesus was certainly with us!"

Lorraine remembered, "We sang the 'Gilligan's Island' song while traveling in those boats. We all laughed and had a great time."

Celing went on with their story. "We knew we wanted to buy land, but I was making only $5 a day from driving people in a jeepney and Lorraine was volunteering at a kindergarten. We had no hope of ever having enough money for land. We went to the United States. We lived in a trailer on Lorraine's dad's land, south of Moriarty, New Mexico. I got a job with a medical supply company, organizing medical supplies. I felt that God really wanted us to go back to the Philippines. I told the company I was quitting. They offered me a big raise to stay. They must have thought I was one of their best workers. But I told them, 'If you offer me a million dollars, I would not be happy if I stayed.'"

Lorraine and Celing returned to the Philippines with their three young ones: Dave Jonathan (fondly called DJ); Micah, on Celing's back in a knapsack, and baby Catherine, who had been born during their stay in New Mexico. The little family flew home. With the money Celing had saved, they bought land near Sariaya. (Only Filipinos can legally buy land.)

Celing and his brothers built the family house. Then they built a boys' house and a girls' house. That was the first orphanage, they lovingly call 'God's training ground.'

As Diana Fogel explained in the biographical book, Desperate For Love, the first orphanage ran into trouble with people who had good intentions, but did not understand or agree with Lorraine's style for raising orphaned, abandoned, abused kids. Lorraine smiles at the amazing blessing God has given them for connecting with most of the grown up children from that first orphanage. Strong bonds of love, even over the years, never fade.

6 RESPECT, RESPONSIBILITY, RESOURCEFULNESS

Proverbs 19:20-21 KJV Hear counsel, and receive instruction,
that thou mayest be wise in thy latter end.
There are many devices in a man's heart; nevertheless
the counsel of the LORD, that shall stand.
Psalm 34:18 KJV The LORD is nigh unto them that are of a broken
heart; and saveth such as be of a contrite spirit.

The Lord brings children to the ranch mainly through the DSWD (Department of Social Welfare and Development). Lorraine continues to contact people she has worked with over the years, in schools, businesses, and state level agencies. Early in her ministry, Lorraine volunteered at the DSWD the state-run orphanage in Lucena City, that houses not only orphaned and abandoned children, but also the elderly with no family to care for them, the mentally ill, and severely disabled people. Most children at FHL come from the DSWD.

When the Lord leads Lorraine to accept a child, she takes pictures of them when they first arrive at the ranch. Most of the children arrive in rags and with parasites in their bodies. But more importantly, their faces reflect the anger, fear, and horrible hurt in their minds and hearts. Then, she takes pictures in about two months of living in a Christ-filled, loving, responsible, environment. In every case, the change is dramatic. The contrast between the frowning, self-protecting, child, to the smiling, healthy, confident kid is nothing less than a miracle.

When the number of children grew from the first three brothers, to about twelve children, Lorraine hired a few staff members to cook and work as caregivers at night. Lorraine laughs at her own lack of cooking skills: rice in the electric rice cooker or 'oatmeal anyone?'

Lorraine chose the ACE curriculum to teach in her classroom. The strength of ACE is that it helps the children read, understand, and write English, as well as to learn the Christian way of living through fictional characters, and Biblical truths. The science, social studies, and math components build on the child's skill at the time they begin and continually strengthen understanding in an orderly fashion.

"In order for children to become successful at the three R's of Reading, 'Riting, 'Rithmetic, they must first learn the three R's of Respect, Responsibility, and Resourcefulness." This simple motto, Lorraine has adopted, not only for herself, but for all the children she has worked with, including their own three.

When the children first come to the ranch, they have next to nothing. Their clothes are usually dirty, ragged, and either grossly too small or too big and they are usually barefooted. People from the USA send boxes of child-sized clothing and shoes. Lorraine fits the children with three sets of school clothes and five sets of play clothes, including underwear. Each child also gets a good pair of flip flops.

Each child has his or her own place to sleep. In the early days they all slept on bamboo mats on the floor, which is the Filipino custom. Not long afterward, Lorraine received money for foam mattresses, pillows, and sheets. Later, the DSWD required individual beds so Celing and his workers built single beds and bunk beds out of wood, along with benches, tables, and bookcases. He could build them much cheaper than buying ready-made furniture and of better quality.

Teaching children to take care of the things they have is the first step in learning responsibility. She taught the children to wash their clothes and dishes at the pump. Chores often become a joyful time of singing and fun. As a rule, older children help the younger children, until they learn the routine.

"Mommy," the children call, as they come to her with hurts as well as joyful accomplishments. Their desire is to hear Mommy say, "Well done," and hug them.

"Look, Mommy, I washed my clothes all by myself!"

Mommy and Daddy's house is the center of everything. Often Mommy has devotions in her living room. When kiddos get sick, they end up on her couches, where Mommy covers shaking bodies, administers medicine, and even wipes up their vomit. Taking care of all their needs, no matter how tired she is, is an important part of being a 'Kid Whisperer!'

Real joy comes with knowing you have done well.

7   SPONTANEITY AS GOD'S HOLY SPIRIT GUIDES

Colossians 1:27-28 KJV To whom God would make known…
which is Christ in you, the hope of glory:
Whom we preach, warning every man, and teaching every manin all
wisdom; that we may present every man perfect in Christ Jesus:

Pastor Oscar: "The difference between a good father
and a bad father is not perfection.
It is the ability to acknowledge mistakes so that their children learn from them."

Mommy Lorraine doesn't always do the expected. She likes to shake things up to get the kids to think. She explains it this way:

"To know what hot is, do you have to experience the cold? To know what is pretty, do you have to see someone ugly? To know what is right, do you have to know what is wrong? This month we are learning about self-discipline. We are doing an experiment tomorrow. Freaky Friday! Freaky, because there will be no rules! We will see who has self-discipline to still follow the rules when they don't have to. Pray for us!! Heheh. I will let you know what the turn out is. Will the good be bad? Will some of the good be better? Will the bad be worse? Or maybe the bad will be better!"

Afterwards, Mommy said, "Amazing what happened! Some good, some bad, some expected things, and some very unexpected things! Most of the kiddos who had been here for a while, had already developed 'self-control.' More problems came from new arrivals. At first, no rules must have felt like freedom. One thing we know for sure: we were all glad when that day ended."

8 LOVE UNCONDITIONALLY

Leviticus 19:34 KJV But the stranger that dwelleth with you shall be unto you as one born among you, and thou shalt love him as thyself; for ye were strangers in the land of Egypt: I am the LORD your God.

Jeremiah 31:3 KJV The LORD hath appeared of old unto me, saying, "Yea, I have loved thee with an everlasting love: therefore with lovingkindness have I drawn thee.

Life is not about ourselves, alone. Real living is about others and loving without thought of ourselves.

Lorraine explains: "The kids come with nothing, usually, except the clothes on their back, and those are usually rags. That's one of the reasons why we take before-and-after pictures for their files. That is one of the jobs of our social worker."

"Every child has been hurt in many ways since they were small. They have been left alone. Most are so skinny, their ribs stick out. Many of our kids have learned to steal food to survive. So when they come here they eat and eat, then they take food and hide it, because they aren't convinced we will feed them again. Sometimes it takes days for some of our kiddos to believe that they can count on three meals every single day."

"Before they can learn to trust us, they have to know that they have enough food, a safe place to stay, and clean clothes. Deep trust comes slowly, just like learning about Jesus and trusting Him takes time."

Lorraine knows the importance of personal time with every child, especially when they first arrive. After a child has been at the ranch for a while, she continues to build that personal relationship which blooms into deep, long-lasting, love.

(Author's note: The following scenario is typical of what happens with new arrivals at FHL. We used the same fictitious names as Diane Fogel used in Desperate For Love.)

Lorraine greeted four little boys in Tagalog, since they spoke no English. She helped them bathe and get dressed in new clothes and new flip flops. The boys were only about two or three years old and skinny. They had been given a good meal of chicken and vegetable soup and rice in the dining hall.

"I am so glad you are here at FHL. All the kiddos on our ranch call me Mommy, because I will love you and take care of you."

Four pairs of dark eyes looked at this fair-skinned lady with long, wavy, brown hair. Her eyes were wide and honest. They hadn't known any adults who spoke to them softly in Tagalog. Most adults they had known swore and yelled at them or ignored them completely, as if they were invisible.

"I want you to be happy here. My first job is to keep you safe and take care of you." She paused and looked at their serious faces. They had not smiled.

"Do you want to live here?"

They nodded their heads.

That night she gently tucked a blanket around each one on his own mattress with a small pillow. Probably this was the first time they had ever slept on mattresses. Little ones, like these four boys, have never slept on anything softer than a bamboo mat or a flattened cardboard box.

The next day, after a filling breakfast of oatmeal, Mommy took them into her own house and sat them on the couch.

"Do you boys still want to stay here at the ranch?" she asked in Tagalog.

They all nodded, still not talking to her.

"If you want to stay," Mommy squatted in front of the four little boys so she was at eye level with them, "you must talk to me. Let me ask you again, do you want to stay here at the ranch?"

"Opo," each little boy said, meaning 'yes.' They looked at each other, then at Mommy and each one smiled. ('Po' is the Filipino term for respect.)

"Will you try your best to follow the rules?"

"What are the rules?" Carlo asked.

"Are the rules hard?" Jared asked.

"The rules are easy," Mommy explained. "The first rule is to obey. If you want your life to be happy here at the ranch and in life, OBEY! If you are kind and obedient, so am I. But if you choose to be stubborn and mean...so am I. Either I teach you to be kind and obedient, or you teach me to be stubborn and mean!"

The little boys looked at her with big eyes.

"So what do you want to do?"

"Be happy," Norton said.

"Obey," Jared said.

"Be kind," Jim said.

Carlo didn't say anything. He reached over and hugged her. Then he said, "Mommy."

Later, Lorraine told the author, "It's a battle of who is stronger and who will win the show-down. Because of my love for the children, if I let them win and have their own way in life, they will be losers in the end. Because I have God's calling and strength on my side, I always win! Hehehe!" she chuckled. Mommy always wins because God always wins… if the child is willing to try.

The only possible way for a child to lose hope is when other well-meaning, but sadly unwise adults try to change circumstances.

She continued. "Love and prayer can move mountains."

Just before nap time she talked to the little boys again. "Obey and play! Disobey, you pay! It is time to rest. You don't have to sleep, but you must stay on your mattress and rest."

Mommy stayed right there with them, making the little boys feel secure. She was quiet, perhaps praying.

Within five minutes, all four, relaxed and their even breathing showed they were asleep. They knew, they no longer had to be afraid.

When they woke up, Lorraine was right there. While the little ones slept, Lorraine had gone to take down her own laundry, which she had washed early in the morning.

Her timing is amazing.

"Hello, my dear ones. I see you weren't sleepy at all!" she joked. In her hands she held two cookies for each of them.

She held out two cookies to Carlo. He took hold of them, but she held them and didn't let go.

Carlo looked at the cookies. Then he looked at Mommy's raised eyebrows.

"Pahingi, Po?" Carlo said in a small voice. That is Tagalog for 'can I have some, ma'am?'

Mommy smiled at him and let go of the cookies.

"Salamat, Po," ('thank you,' in Tagalog) Carlo said without being prompted.

"Pahingi, po!" Norton, Jared, and Jim said, with enthusiasm.

They all giggled.

She handed them the cookies and they said, "Salamat, Po!"

"Are you ready for rule number 2?" Mommy asked in Tagalog.

All four boys nodded, looking at her, their eyes wide. They were starting to trust this new adult in their lives.

"The second rule is: Respect yourself, the staff, and others. You reap what you sow. What you plant, you grow! Do you understand what that means?"

"Be good?" Carlo asked, hesitantly.

"That's a good beginning," she said.

"What do you do when you are hungry?" she asked.

"Eat!" said Jared with a big grin.

"That's right," Mommy said. "And what do you do when you are all dirty from playing?"

"Take a bath?" Jim answered, like it was a question.

"Yes, good answer, Jim." Mommy hugged the little boy. "So eating and taking a bath is showing respect for yourself. So how do you respect others?"

"Take them a bath?" Carlo asked, wrinkling his nose.

"No, sweet boy!" Mommy laughed. "Respecting others is like the first rule, obeying the first time you are told…and even better, helping them do something without being told."

"But, I can't," Norton said.

"Come with me, and I will show you." Mommy got up and they followed her to the water pump. "Now who thinks they are strong enough to pump the water?"

All four boys shouted, "Me!"

"Good, I'm glad you are such strong boys. So we will test you. Carlo and Jared, you each get two buckets from over there and put one under the pump." She pointed to buckets lined up on the cement pad. "Jim, you try first."

The little boy had to jump to grab the end of the handle. The handle came down, but no water came out.

"Okay, Jared, you try."

Jared had to jump, just like Jim had. He leaned all of his four-year old weight on the handle. It slowly came down. But, again, no water came out.

"Let me help you get it started," Mommy said. She pumped with one hand several times to get the water started, then she backed away.

"Now, Jared and Jim, work together and both of you grab the handle."

The two skinny little boys with their black hair standing straight up, like scrub brushes, pulled the handle down, again and again! Finally, water ran in a steady stream into the bucket until it was about half full.

"Now let's see if Carlo can pump by himself."

Carlo's eyes were slanted, and his build was more like a Chinese warrior than that of a typical Filipino. He grabbed the handle. The handle didn't budge.

"Norton, please help Carlo," Mommy asked.

Norton was the smallest of all the boys, but he jumped on the handle beside Carlo, and with his weight added to Carlo's, the handle came down and water gushed into the second bucket. The boys took turns pumping, until all four buckets were half full.

"Now we must take the water to the CR." (The CR stands for Comfort Room. The CR is a little room that contains a toilet and a bucket with a dipper. Americans call it the bathroom or restroom.)

Each little boy lifted a bucket and carried it in the direction of the boys' CR. Water sloshed about like little boats in a storm.

"Oh, my," Mommy said. "We won't have any water left, doing it this way. Do you have any ideas?"

"You could help us?" Jared suggested with a question.

"Think about rule number two," Mommy said. "Respect yourself and others. Do you see anyone else struggling?"

The four little boys nodded and looked at each other. They set the buckets on the ground.

"Norton and Jared, you both pick up one bucket. Jim and Carlo, pick up another bucket. I will get in the middle with two buckets. Jared and Carlo hold the handle of my buckets. Now, we all pick up a bucket with two people per bucket."

They each shared the handle of a heavy bucket with the boy next to them and Mommy in the middle. She had to bend her knees to keep the two buckets level for Carlo and Jared. Together, they carried the buckets to the CR with very little sloshing. Together they dumped the water into the barrel.

When they finished, Lorraine sat on the grass with the four little boys.

"Now, what do you think of rules one and two?" Mommy asked the four little boys. "We call it the Golden Rule in action!"

"Mabuti!" (Good!) all four boys said together.

Later, Lorraine explained to me, "In the Philippines they call it 'karma'! What you do to others, comes back to you, good or bad!"

"Are you ready for the third rule?" Mommy asked.

"Opo," (Yes) the boys answered, respectfully.

"This rule is very important," Mommy said seriously. "You must ask permission for everything, from climbing a tree to needing to use the CR. We care about you, and we need and want to know where you are and what you are doing all the time. We are responsible for your life because God has entrusted you to us," she said seriously.

The little boys were quiet.

"Can you ask permission?" Mommy asked.

"Opo," Carlo, Norton, and Jim said.

"What happens if we forget?" Jared asked quietly.

"I'm glad you asked that. You are such smart boys," Mommy answered. She smiled. She reached into her pocket and took out eight plastic bracelets.

"These are Behavior Bracelets. You each get two," she said. The little boys took two bracelets of different colors. They put them on.

"You have bracelets on, too, Mommy," Jared said. "But you have many?"

"Yes, I do," she said. She showed them her wrists. "I took these extra bracelets away from kiddos who did not follow the rules."

Carlo put the two bracelets on then shook his hand. The bracelets fell right off. "Uh oh," he said. "If I play, my bracelets will fall off."

"Let me show you a trick," Mommy said.

She took his bracelets and twisted them one inside the other. Then she slid the looped bracelets onto his wrist. He shook his arm. The bracelets stayed on.

"Mabuti?" she asked.

He shook his wrist. "Mabuti," he said with a smile.

Mommy helped Norton, Jared, and Jim twist their bracelets together so they would stay on their small wrists.

"Do you like them?" she asked.

"Opo," they answered.

"Do you want to keep them?" she asked.

"Opo," they answered.

"Then follow the rules, my darlings," she said. She took their hands and looked at them seriously. "Are you sure you want to keep your bracelets?"

"Opo, Mommy," they said.

"There is a fun way to help you remember to obey and respect rules. Your bracelet can be called a 'band' also. So if you want to obey and respect, repeat after me," she said.

Mommy said each line and the four little boys repeated after her: "B – bad words
A – attitude (anger)

N – not telling the truth

D – disobedience

S – stealing"

Mommy hugged those four little boys and she walked them to the gym to play. She introduced them to the care-giver in charge of watching the younger children.

"Now, you follow the rules with her, just like with me. Can you do that?" She leaned over and looked each boy in the eyes.

"Opo," all four answered, seriously.

As we walked back to her house, Lorraine explained, "I keep the bracelets for just one day or up to week, depending on the age of the child and the severity of the infraction."

Proverbs 15:1 KJV A soft answer turneth away wrath: but grievous words stir up anger.

Lorraine's system of discipline works wonders. Lorraine never yells. She is more likely to whisper in a child's ear. In the evenings after school and chores, Lorraine and Celing sit outside where the children are playing or reading. Sometimes they comb, braid, and style hair. The older children have learned to cut hair. They laugh, play, sing, dance, play tag, throw balls, jump rope, skate, or just sit quietly and talk. It is a magical time. Children and adults feel the unconditional love. Deep bonding takes place. It is family time in the true sense, even including visitors and staff.

9 SIMPLE LIFE, SIMPLE PROBLEMS

"Simple Life, simple problems!" Lorraine says quite often. And her life reflects a simple life, and simple solutions to problems before they become big problems.

"The water pump is the center of every home and small community," Lorraine points out. Lorraine and Celing met at the water pump, when they were young, doing the simple task of washing their clothes.

Dishes, baths, clothes, and brushing teeth all take place at the pump. Buckets must be filled and taken to the CR. After going to the toilet, most Filipinos have no use for toilet paper…a few little splashes of water on the bottom, pour water into the toilet to wash it down, then dip water over your hands…and the job is done! There is no messy, expensive toilet paper, or paper towels. The water droplets dry quickly in the warm air…SIMPLE.

Several FHL supporters have offered to pay for an electric pump, and water tank, but pumps for running water require electricity. Often in rural areas, the power is not consistent. Pumps often go out when the electricity fluctuates.

"At our first orphanage, they installed an electric motor and pump and large holding tank. I would lay awake at night hearing that pump going off and on. I worried that there was water left on and running somewhere," Lorraine commented. "I couldn't sleep, so I had to get up and check all the spigots. I determined not to have that here." She laughed. "And…I sleep much better."

"We tried a pump for the guest house here for a while," Celing explained. "But the pump kept burning out and then the guests were upset because there was no running water. It's better to teach our guests the Filipino way right from the start. Then when the electricity goes out, the guests are not disappointed by not having what they didn't have in the first place!" Celing laughed.

"Simple life, simple problems," Lorraine said again. We all laughed.

On the ranch, Lorraine has a bell for boys' bath time and later a bell for girls' bath time. The children know that when it is not their bath time they stay away from the pump area. They soap their hair then their body leaving their shorts on. Then they pour dippers of cold water from the pump over their heads to wash the soap away. They laugh and splash each other. Then they dry with towels, wrap the towels around them and hurry to their rooms to get dressed for bed.

Doing laundry at the pump, I learned by experience, must follow certain steps. When we went to FHL Ranch the first time, the children taught me how to wash clothes. Of course, the kids watched to see how efficient I was!

The first step is to fill four, large, plastic tubs with water, bucket by bucket from the pump. Pumping the water itself takes a lot of energy and stamina. Lifting the handle is fairly easy. Pulling the handle down, takes strength and perseverance. To repeat the action, over and over, in order to get a steady stream of water to fill a tub is a real challenge. The smallest children took great joy in showing me how fast they could pump. I made a poor competitor. The kids shook their heads and took over pumping to fill my wash tubs. They pumped so fast, and filled four tubs so quickly, it was almost as if there were an electric pump.

First, clothes are put into the first tub to soak. Powder soap is put into the second tub and each article of clothing is put into the bubbly water, one at a time, after squeezing some of the water out of each one. Then, the hard work starts. Each piece of clothing must be dipped in the water and scrubbed vigorously between the clenched hands. This action is done over and over: neck, sleeves, back and front. If there is a particularly dirty spot, especially in white clothes, a bit of bleach, mixed with water in a bottle can be used. The next step is to wring the excess soapy water out and put it into the next tub for rinsing out soap. When you get a good number of clothes in the third tub, slosh and rinse…slosh and rinse. Squeeze and add to the fourth tub of fresh water. The next step is to dip and squeeze, dip and squeeze. If the water is still soapy, you need a fifth tub.

Lorraine laughed at me when I had trouble getting all the soap out. She said, "If it rains when you're wearing your clothes, you will be covered in bubbles and float away!" We both laughed and one of the children pumped another tub of water for me, to rinse again.

The most difficult step is to wring the water out of towels, pants, and sheets. The last step is to hang the clothes on the line with clothes pins. It helps to hang the clothes on a line under a roof because of the frequent rain. At a later visit, we were delighted to see that Celing had purchased a spinner for heavier clothes like towels.

Celing and his crew have built two cabins and a duplex for guests. Each has a private bathroom, complete with a toilet, a sink and a barrel of water. Guests at the ranch must learn the simple method of bathing like the kids with soap and a bucket of cold water. All the water is cold, but that is okay because the climate is warm and wet in the winter, and warmer and drier in the summer. But, it you bathe in the morning, the cold water gives a bit of a wake-up shock. Brrr! Morning baths are quick, indeed.

The kids help us fill our guest bathroom barrel. The children shower in the evening, after a sweaty day of school, chores, and playing. Sometimes we shower twice a day, just to cool off.

One evening we were sitting in the gym with the children. Some were skating, two boys were shooting baskets, and two little girls were sitting on a stack of chairs, reading, because they had no bands. Two boys were sitting on another stack of chairs for the same reason. Four older girls were chatting with Mommy and Daddy. Two were combing and styling Lorraine's hair.

A bell clanged, sounding like a cow bell.

"Bath time, boys," Lorraine said in a normal voice. She never yells, even with so much noise going on. The kids know Mommy's voice.

Immediately, the boys put away the ball and the skates and went to get their towels and clean clothes. The two little boys, who had no bracelets, climbed down from the stack of chairs and came over to Mommy.

She wrapped her arms around them and ruffled their hair. Then she whispered something in their ears.

"Thank you, Mommy," they chimed. They grinned and climbed back up on the chairs with their books.

"Whatever you said, made them happy," I commented.

"They don't need to take a bath tonight, because they haven't been playing hard today to get all sweaty. You see how happy they are. Sometimes losing their bracelets for discipline has its perks. Hehehe!"

"Look, Mommy! How do you like it?" The girls, who had been styling her hair, handed her a mirror. They had made her normal pony tail into a bun, fastened with a hair tie and brushed her bangs high and fluffy above her forehead.

Lorraine took the mirror and looked this way and that. Then she put her arms around them both. "You two are elegant hair dressers!"

As the years went by, and the first FHL children became teenagers, it became necessary for more privacy for bath time. Celing built a separate bath house with concrete walls separating the boys' side from the girls' side.

None of the children have cell phones or electronic games. They play chess and other board games. Boys and girls play dodge ball, ping pong, baseball, touch football, and basketball. They use jump ropes, skates, skateboards, and bicycles. They fly kites, jump, run, bounce on the trampoline, cross monkey bars, and have fun in unlimited creative ways.

When groups from churches or other organizations come to visit and help, Lorraine has the visitors sit down and talks to them and their leaders about rules. Then she has the leaders collect all their electronic devices. Mommy Lorraine is serious about 'Simple life, Simple problems.'

10   BUILDING TO LAST

Concrete is the best building material in the Philippines because it doesn't melt in the rain or blow away in typhoons.

Celing and a crew of local men, and sometimes a short term missionary crew from Australia, along with some of the older ranch boys, most recently, have built a Bible School at the far end of the ranch.

It was amazing to watch them, laughing and joking, as they shoveled bags of cement and rocks into the electric cement mixer. After it was well mixed, one of the boys helped dump the heavy wet cement into buckets. Joyfully, they tossed one heavy bucket at a time to the next man in line, closer to the area it was needed for the walls, and then the floor. The most skilled men smoothed the cement into place. Celing is not only the designer, but the most skilled in fashioning the concrete buildings. He puts the finishing touches with decorative tile on the floors, around windows and doors, and along the walls for a very professional look.

"I try to keep the crew happy by joking and talking. A happy crew works better and faster. A little competition helps, too. So far, nobody can beat me! But that day will come!" Celing raised his eyebrows. "It's the same with kids. When they laugh and have fun while they work, then the job doesn't seem like work. We build to last: buildings, as well as kids."

The kids helped with cement outside their house. The new cement pad made a nicer place for washing and drying clothes, especially after the roof was added. And they learned a skill they could use later in life.

11   DISCIPLINE IS THE KEY TO SUCCESS

Proverbs 22:6 KJV Train up a child in the way he should go: and when he is old, he will not depart from it.

Mommy Lorraine knows that discipline is the key to success and she puts that wisdom into practice every minute of every day. When discipline by others becomes self-discipline, there is victory.

Lorraine explains, "The other kiddos who have been here the longest are the best teachers. Simple things like getting in line for meals, washing up after using the CR, and brushing their teeth after meals, are all first steps they learn by copying the older kids. That all started with DJ, Micah, and Catherine."

Exercises and running before a meal reminds the kids that their bracelets are important. Discipline becomes fun with Mommy!

Lorraine understands that maturity comes when a child knows what must be done and does it without being told.

"Losing their bracelet is a reminder that they are loved! We tell them by correcting and disciplining them, it's a sign that we care enough to take the time to deal with their weaknesses and want to turn them into strengths. If they accept and admit their sins, the strike or discipline, is shortened and rewarded for having a happy heart, during correction."

"ATTITUDE IS EVERYTHING HERE! When they admit right away their sins, sometimes there is no discipline at all, because they were brave enough to come forth right away and confess. But that is a rare case. Hehehe. What we started to do 2 years ago is to give them a clearance. After a half day or whole day of 'no play, extra chores, read books,' depending on their age and sin, they must have their teacher, leader, or caregiver sign their reprieve, which means there is no issue with the child for the rest of the day. After it has been signed, and the teacher, leader, or caregiver prays with the child, THEN he or she goes to my house for the last signature. Hehehe. Then I let them pray and they receive their band."

"At the end of the day, if they haven't received their bands, they must run as many laps as their age. They run around the basketball court or around the dining hall. Receiving a popsicle stick for every lap as a counter. Once they have collected the number of their age, they are done and give the sticks back to me. Even 4 year olds can run 4 laps. When our kids join Fun Runs, guess what?? YES! They win! 1st, 2nd 3rd places. Hehehe! That is turning SIN into WIN! And RUN into FUN! Also the kids with lots of strikes are our best readers because that is all they can do after extra chores: is to read books, until their clearance is signed and they get their band back.

"We give the kids allowance each week. They can spend their money for extra snacks, or save it to take to town when we go, if they have had no strikes for a month. The kids earn coins in school. Every morning they get three pesos on their office shelf. It they still have three pesos at the end of the day for following the rules, they can save them up to use in the school store to buy a small toy or a special school supply like a mechanical pencil."

See, Mommy, I got my bands back!

Mommy gives out rewards.

BEHAVIOR BANDS
Get creative with discipline
Discipline comes from the word 'disciple'
(Follower of Jesus) – BEHAVIOR BANDS

B   bad words

A   attitude/anger

N   not telling the truth

D   disobedience

S   stealing

S   sleep early (go to bed with no play)

T   TV banned without a band

R   running their age helps with rage

I   increase their chores so they don't get bored

K   keep reading

E   end of play for the day

Let your YES, be YES and your NO be NO,
like it says in Matthew 5:37.
"Say what you mean, and mean what you say.
If a child can pass my oral quiz they get a free band!"

No band still brings a smile in class with a cooling fan and computer practice.

One band is a good reminder to be careful to keep privileges in-tact!

12 TEAMS

Team work is vital to Lorraine's management system and training. Older students, who have been at the ranch and know the routine, make excellent team leaders. These leaders listen to the younger students read and help with math and writing. Mommy Lorraine knows that good education is vital to ensure that as the children step out on their own, they will have a chance at a better life than they had before they came to the ranch. Team leaders are given the opportunity to practice people skills. Mommy teaches leadership.

Mommy explains. "When a child has proven that they can be trusted, I make them a team leader of four or five other children, some younger, some older. Depending on the number of children living on the ranch, there may be four to eight teams. I pray with the leaders. Then I assign a job for the leader to do with their team: sweeping leaves, cleaning and mopping the dining hall, cleaning the CR, cleaning the gym, taking care of the gardens, washing dishes, cleaning the pump area, cleaning the Bible School, and sometimes I give the team a list of people and problems to pray for. I like to mix things up so nobody gets bored."

"Group leaders make choices for their group. I talk with them and listen to them about how their decisions turned out. Then I listen to the team members. I help each leader evaluate how their decisions as a leader worked and then make changes. I listen to them and ask how they could do it better. I don't tell them. Experience is the best teacher. Quite often, I choose a child who may not be quite ready, but I want to give them the experience of having others depend on them. It is interesting to watch a child rise to the challenge."

"A child may not have any idea how to lead, but that is the beauty of the system. Being chosen as a leader helps them feel important. They know they must think of others. They must be accountable for each member. I pray with them. They pray for their team members. They learn to work with the others on their team, not just telling them what to do, but working along with them. A big part of being a team leader is to listen to the others, encourage them, create a little competition, and help each other."

Mommy Lorraine is a perfect example. No job is too small. Mommy leads by doing every job with the kids. Mommy pumps water, just like they do. She helps do laundry with the little ones. She sweeps leaves with a bamboo broom, dumps the leaves in a wheelbarrow, and wheels it to the concrete pit where it will be burned. The key is to have fun while working. We have seen the kids laughing and singing along with Mommy while they are doing dishes in plastic pans together. Mommy occasionally brings out big plastic wading pools on hot days, and she gets as wet as the little ones do! Mommy is in the middle of the activities, all day long, and well into the night.

It is so natural to see Mommy Lorraine doing different activities with the teams.

When it is school time, in the early years, Lorraine spent all day in the classroom, also.

Now she is able to hire people, several of whom have been faithful teachers over the years. Sometimes, volunteers come to work in the school, like Larry and I have for a couple of months over a period of four years.

Over the years, Lorraine has had several young people who have come from the United States. Some have stayed for six months or more. Most volunteers receive twice the blessings they intend to give and learn a good deal about themselves and their own personal relationship with the Lord Jesus Christ.

The importance of being consistent in the classroom, at play, and for caregivers at night is vital.

Larry I have seen teams work well. Two different years, we planned a treasure hunt using directional compasses. We taught the kids how to use the compasses, then we laid out seven different courses with compass directions. We gave each team leader the first clue with part of a Bible verse. The leaders had to keep their team together and help the members cooperate to find the clues. When they found the last part of their verse, they all returned to Mommy and said the complete Bible verse. The team leaders had quite a job keeping the team together!

Doing things together, makes even jumping from a big bouncy branch, more fun.

The trampoline, donated by supporters, is not necessarily an individual activity. It has become the focal point of many video dramas filmed by the kids.

Teachers, Leaders, and Caregivers all together, equals lots of TLC...Tender, Loving, Care!

13 CHOICES

"Before kids can learn the three R's of Readin', 'Rritin', and 'Rithmetic,
they must learn to be Respectful, Responsible, and Resourceful!

1. Amazing opportunity: Children walk out of being abandoned and abused into amazing opportunity.
2. Choosing change: Children have a chance to choose between their past and everything Jesus Christ and FHL have to offer.
3. Forgiving or Fighting: Children choose between Forgiving and Forgetting the rejection and abuse of their past, or they can choose to Fight and Flee from Mommy and Daddy and most importantly from God.
4. Choosing Jesus: Admitting their sins and asking Jesus to help them do better is difficult and takes time.

Proverbs 11:2 KJV (Paraphrased)
When pride (comes), then comes shame;
But with the lowly is wisdom.

Lorraine explains: "Once a child grasps understanding of respect by obeying those in authority, following simple rules, taking care of themselves, and helping others, then they are ready for responsibility. Being responsible is doing their fair share, being honest, and helping others without being told. The more responsibility a child takes on, the more they learn to be resourceful. Being resourceful is figuring out how to cook, clean, encourage others when you don't feel like it, and solve problems with what you have. After a child proves they are respectful, responsible, and resourceful, then they are ready to seriously learn to read, write, and do math in our school. None of this learning has to do with age. Some mature faster than others."

"When little children have been left alone, starved, hurt mentally, physically, and emotionally, it seems there is no other choice as they grow older, except to repeat the same patterns. Left alone, most people do repeat the sins of the past," Lorraine explains sadly.

But Mommy Lorraine and Daddy Celing have proved over and over in the lives of so many children, that when they change the circumstances and teach them how to be: RESPECTFUL, learn to take RESPONSIBILITY, and become RESOURCEFUL, then most children have the 'everlasting hope' promised in 2nd Thessalonians 2:16, so that they can make a better life for themselves. Then they have gained the ability to do so with the help of Jesus Christ.

Mommy and Daddy show by their own lives that they can do all things through Jesus Christ as applied from Philippians 4:13.

Lorraine and Celing have had to take these very steps in meeting challenges from paid workers on the ranch, visitors from other countries and other towns, as well as ever-changing government regulations.

These three young ladies are now independent.
Each one stays in close contact with Mommy.

14   UNCOMPROMISING LOVE
COMMITMENT FOR THE LONG RUN

Matthew 5:44 KJV But I say unto you, Love your enemies, bless them that curse you, do good to them that hate you, and pray for them which despitefully use you, and persecute you;

2GET and 2GIVE cause problems.
To solve problems, double it
4 GET and 4 GIVE

We know from the book of James, chapter 2, that faith without works is dead! You have put your faith into action and God has blessed it! To Him be the glory forever! Amen.

Lorraine wrote this encouraging thought about the year 2016: Live each day as if it were your last! You just never know what's around the corner. This has been an incredible year with so many blessings that we could hardly contain. Is it the calm before the storm?? God, whatever you allow to happen, we know YOU are in control and our life is in YOUR hands. Read and apply Psalm 23!

Uncompromising love is deeply challenging as kids leave. When Lorraine and Celing accept children into their lives, they become Mommy and Daddy in every way. They treat the children just like the three they gave birth to. The new children become part of the family. Mommy and Daddy simply expand their hearts. A serious commitment is made before God for the life of each child, both present and future. Unfortunately, when the government and/or certain individuals interfere with the plan, the hopes and dreams for becoming successful, loving adults does not always happen.

Celing and his workers built three concrete trash pits about 18 feet deep, 12 feet by 15 feet long. One pit is for material that will decompose into good mulch. A second pit is for material that can burn. The third pit is for materials made of cardboard, plastic, glass, or metal that can be recycled. Several enterprising older people collect such materials and sell them by the pound to collection centers.

Baby chicks learn about kitchen scraps early. Turkeys
like to roost on the wall for relative safety

Chickens and turkeys have free range on the ranch. One day as I took our trash to the pits, I noticed a teenaged chicken in the pit. I was so concerned that the chicken would die in the pit, that I looked for Celing to rescue the poor chicken. He looked at me and shook his head. I was surprised by his lack of compassion.

But this is the story he told me about that chicken:

"For some reason, that chicken fell into the pit, which was half full of trash so I put a long board sticking out so the chicken could climb out itself and join its family. I left it there for three days, but the chicken was still in the pit. So I climbed down the board myself and gently lifted it up to the bank. But when I came back a little later, that chicken had jumped back into the pit. I had left the board there, so I climbed back into the pit, gently picked up that confused chicken, and carried it back to the place most of the chickens like to hang out by the kitchen, where they get free food from scraps the cook throws out. We try not to waste anything on the ranch. Two days later, some of the kids came and told me there was a chicken in the pit. I was about to burn the burnable trash, so I went, and there was that same chicken, back in the pit. This time I put the chicken in a bag and took it to the far side of the ranch and let it go. I told that chicken that if it didn't stay away from the pit, it would end up being roast chicken. Well, it stayed away a whole week, until after I had finished burning. Then the very next day, that stubborn chicken had found its way back, and what do you think? It jumped right back into the pit."

"Now, you know that chicken was a teenager, and just like kids when they get to be teenagers, they think they know everything. Even when God rescues them and puts them here on the ranch with safety, good food, and lots of love, some of them just crave getting back into the world's pit of evil. And until they get sick of the results of their choices, and allow our Lord Jesus to help them change their mind and heart, they just keep returning to the pit, just like that chicken."

Celing, with firewood he has chopped, is standing
beside the teen-aged chicken's favorite concrete pit

Children come to FHL sometimes for a few weeks and sometimes for years. We knew one little girl who came for three weeks, then her birth mother came to the ranch, and took her to Manila to live with a new boyfriend. Sometimes, being reunited with family members works out for good, but in most cases, the children simply return to the same deplorable conditions they had escaped for a while.

One ten-year old boy, whose behavior was incorrigible, was sent from another orphanage to the ranch, to see if Lorraine could help him learn to be respectful and to take responsibility for basic chores. The hope was that he could change enough to be permanently adopted by a nice family. He seemed happy at first, but as days went by, he totally did the opposite of what he was told or ignored the rules, requests and chores completely. He climbed up on the roofs of buildings, and was rude, even to Lorraine.

One day, I asked him, "Why do you do such naughty things?"

He replied, "Because I can. Who is going to stop me?"

He was sent back to his original orphanage, with no hope of adoption, unless our Lord Jesus intervened, of course. There is always hope.

When children have the opportunity to stay at the ranch long enough to see hope of a new future for themselves with Jesus Christ leading, they desire to go on to college or a trade school, or to get a good job with the skills they have learned on the ranch. Often, with the training they get with Daddy Celing in practical building skills, a few of the boys are able to get construction jobs outside of the ranch.

Lorraine and Celing's original plan was to raise children, family-style into young adult-hood. Unfortunately, the government of the Philippines made new laws that orphanages could not keep children for longer than six months, or a year at the most. As a result, many of the kids had to go back to family, where they were once again left to their own devices.

Most of the kids who have lived at the ranch for several years, keep in close touch with Mommy and Daddy, because that relationship is the deepest family tie they have ever experienced. Several come back to visit the ranch, some with their own children. Facebook has proven to be a wonderful social networking tool. Even when the children move away from the Philippines, they are able to stay in touch with Mommy and Daddy.

But some are like the chicken in the trash pit. They fall into a sad life style. Some try to ask for money from the grown FHL kids who have gone on to school and have good jobs. Others, even after Celing or Micah help them get a good job, mess up and blame the very ones who help them. We know that our Lord Jesus is merciful, but He also lets the rebellious ones who refuse to accept His way of working hard and putting others first, to have their own way.

We continue to pray for those precious ones to return to Jesus and truly make Him real in their lives.

Lorraine wrote, "Our greatest treasures are our kids. Invest in them, all that you can and someday you will reap the harvest. Single mothers are important to us. Half of our staff positions are single moms. Most single moms are not only mothers, but also the only bread-winners for their families.

I know many sweet and incredible parents out there who watched their kids go in a different direction than they had hoped for. I could never understand that, until it happened to me. It's the worst pain that I know of. But God in His mercies will restore, recover, and regain our strength once again. We hope in what we don't see and that is true faith! (Hebrews 11:1) Never give up praying for His perfect time."

"Faith is the basis of why we are here. When we read about the miracles that Jesus performed, we see very simple gestures and spoken words, with unwavering faith attached to them. Jesus either touched people or spoke a few words, and healing took place. God is present to meet our every need. He is looking for OUR FAITH to combine with HIS LOVE to grant our deepest desires. There is much to be learned in FAITH. Read the Bible every day, pray, and believe. Watch for the verbs! God is telling us to do something!"

Matthew 9:2-7 (Jesus healed the man sick with palsy. He told him to pick up his bed and walk.) Keep it simple!

Luke 2:20 (The shepherds, after they saw baby Jesus, were praising and glorifying God!) Tell everyone about Jesus!

Matthew 15:22-28 (A woman was persistent in asking Jesus to heal her daughter.) Pray! Have FAITH! Jesus answers!

15 NEW BEGINNINGS

Lorraine is no stranger to new beginnings. She has learned that God always has His purpose in every change whether it be through government, or hurtful individuals.

"Now we are doing more babies, it is more encouraging. Our first baby has been adopted by a family in Spain and another one will soon be adopted by a family in France. We have the opportunity to get these young ones ready for a year. A group of four siblings got adopted together in the United States. I really think this is the way to go! What joyful possibilities!"

"My soul rests quietly when it looks to God."

Psalm 62:1 KJV Truly my soul waiteth upon God: from him cometh my salvation.

The government is getting better about many things. Lorraine posted in October, 2016: "Left the ranch at 3:30 a.m. to face the day I dreaded the most. I had to renew my Visa I-card for another five years so I can stay in the Philippines and not be TNT (hiding from Immigration). Five years ago, when I went to Immigration in Manila, it was the worst day of my life. It started at 8:00 a.m. and finished at 5:00 p.m. going from window to window, paying for every receipt. Paying with an extra 500 pesos rush fee was common for every receipt for my 3 kids and me. We left frustrated, exhausted, and broke. Yesterday was a different story. People were actually nice and happy. We went in at 7:40 a.m. and got out at 10:a.m. FINISHED! No more rush fee! Heheheh! One receipt to pay! Extra money to go out and eat to celebrate! Who do I thank for these changes? We thank God, as well as, our newly elected Filipino president, Duterte. I am so grateful for the clean-up he has done around the Philippines in such a short time. Not only are things better with medicines, but also in these government offices. I am proud to be married to a Filipino and have the privilege of living in this beautiful country. Hats off to you, Mr. President. God bless, protect and keep you safe, strong, and full of wisdom!!"

Zig Ziglar said it in a nutshell, "The past cannot be changed, forgotten, edited, or erased. It can only be accepted." And we might add, "You can either build on your past to improve your life with the help of Jesus Christ, or blame your past and jump back into it."

****

Grace was one of the first children we met at the ranch. She made us feel special. She and Ronny, a boy with a heart as big as his smile, were the first to show us around. At the end of our 2 1/2 months at the ranch, Larry and I awarded these two pre-teens special awards, 'Most Congenial.' We were also delighted by Grace's little three-year old sister, who was quite precocious. Lorraine took us on a visit to DSWD, where hundreds of children live, sometimes for years, after being taken off the streets, or left by mothers who feel they can no longer provide for their children. We met Grace's little brother, who had spent some time on the ranch but proved to be so incorrigible, he had to be returned to DSWD. Grace hugged her younger brother with tears and a gift she had made for him. Lorraine greeted him as well. He acted restless, and didn't even stay long to talk to Grace.

Now, after several years of our visits, Grace has become even more special to us. She, along with Bek x2 (Larry's nickname for the other little girl in the picture) showed us their favorite things: the 'shy plant' that curls up its leaves when touched, wild berries, and what to do if we are caught in the rain without an umbrella.

Umbrellas are important, rain or shine!

One evening, Grace brought a tiny gecko egg she had found behind a picture frame. She was hoping to watch it hatch. Grace has a deep sense of wonder that Larry and I truly admire.

Grace is one child who was given the opportunity to live and grow on the ranch for several years. Mommy Lorraine has impacted Grace's life in countless ways.

In October, 2016, Grace wrote her story. Here it is in part:

"My name is Mary Grace and I am 20 years old. My life was like a big storm. I grew up in a broken family. My life was miserable with no direction. My mother had 17 children with 10 different men. I was one of those beggars on the street. I was 2 years old and my brother was 1. The group we roamed with went around begging for food and money. We slept in jeeps and on the streets. My mother was with us, too, until we got separated. Then we were picked up and taken to the DSWD. We lived there for 8 years, just wards of the government, with not a single person to love us or even care. I took care of my brother, until one day, my brother was gone. All I knew was that he was at Faith, Hope, and Love Kids Ranch. I got so angry that I gave the staff a hard time and didn't eat for 3 days. I told them that I wouldn't listen or eat until they sent my brother back to me. The staff had to do something, so they did the best thing ever: they called Mommy Lorraine and told her about me, and that she had my brother."

"They took me to FHL to join my brother. At first I was stubborn and naughty. I did not follow the rules, and did everything I wanted. After a month of being disciplined, and loved, little-by-little, my attitude changed. I realized Mommy and Daddy did not hurt children, and made us feel safe. My brother, sadly for me, didn't understand and had to go back to DSWD."

"After two years, I saw my mom on the street with my youngest sister, who was only about three years old. I prayed that somehow my mom would bring her to the ranch. God answered my prayer. Mommy Lorraine and Daddy Celing loved us and treated us like their own children. They home-schooled us and taught us the Word of God. I stayed at the ranch for almost six years. But then the government said I had to go live with a relative."

"We were supposed to be put up for adoption, but my mother wouldn't sign the papers. She visited us at the ranch a few times. I was getting to old to be adopted anyway. Then the government made a law that said we had to go back to whatever family we could. My older brother, that I didn't even know, invited us to live with him in Batangas, two hours away. That's where I met Carlo, the man who is now my husband, and his family. Together we had our baby boy, Gabriel, and a year later, our baby girl, Carla Jane. Together, we tried to stay healthy and strong. But I knew something was missing."

"After four years of being away from the ranch, I decided to call Mommy Lorraine. I wanted to try to fix all my mistakes. Mommy Lorraine told me she had been praying for me and would be glad to talk to me. She invited us to the Christmas party at the ranch. I went with my little sister and my two little ones. Mommy and Daddy offered to let us come to the ranch to live and work. I went back to Batangas, excited to go, but Carlo did not agree. I kept on praying. Then one day, unexpectedly, Carlo agreed to go with me to the ranch." Carlo and I were married in the Bible School. Daddy Celing built us a small house, and I am going to school to get my high school diploma. It is the greatest time for us. I am blessed to be able to fix my life and move on with Jesus and the Lamar's, and my FHL family. By God's amazing grace, we will live happily ever after!"

16 WHERE GOD GUIDES, GOD PROVIDES

Lorraine and Celing are very matter-of-fact about the business end of running FHL.

"Money for missionaries is always a problem. The more young ones to feed and clothe, the more money is required. Staff must be paid. The electric and phone bills must be paid. The jeepney and van gas tanks must stay filled. Laundry soap, toothpaste, shampoo, and other personal items all cost money. Inspectors found the well water not up to code for drinking, so now we buy our drinking water in five-gallon jugs."

"I found a dentist who would give the children free dental work. But doctors and medicine require immediate cash and there is no health insurance."

"No matter what the income is, God provides enough good food for the kids, staff, and visitors. Everyone always eats well. Most of the food comes from local fish and rice vendors. Celing and the kids plant vegetables and fruit trees as well as flowers. I buy whole chickens from the markets in Lucena City."

Celing explains, "I manage the money and pay all the bills. Even though sometimes it seems that there is never quite enough money. But, at the end of the day, there is always enough in the bank to cover every need. Sometimes visitors or those who support us feel the leading of the Holy Spirit to give us a certain amount. Time after time, what they give is just the amount we need to buy medicine or pay a doctor or hospital bill. Our great God knows our needs before we do."

"We make sure no single donor provides for FHL. Most of our support comes from a few churches, but mostly from individuals we have met over the years. God has brought people from all over the world to support FHL. God puts into their hearts to give what they can, and then many come to visit. We truly believe God is guiding us, and He truly is providing."

Making funny faces, eating outside, enjoying the variety of food, makes everyone happy. Even our granddaughter, Becky, enjoyed the crunchy fish.

Helping in the kitchen doesn't seem like a chore when samples are at hand. Certain tree leaves add spice to soup.

Celing enjoys talking about food. "I have tried raising pigs, but they are too much work for what they are worth. We still buy a pig to slaughter every few months. I built a greenhouse to raise vegetables and flowers all year. We recently got our tilapia ponds up and running. We get healthy fish of about 12 to 14 inches long. God wants us to do everything we can to help ourselves."

"We buy cows that are pregnant, and then when the calf is born, we have milk for the kids and a calf to fatten up. Most of the cattle on the ranch are steers. We raise them, and then sell them, to help pay unexpected expenses. One of the boys, Chris, who had been with us at our first orphanage, came to live at FHL. He had earned enough money to buy his own steer. He raised it, helped with milking, and became a caregiver for the little boys, to pay for his room and board. He sold the steer to pay for his college.

"There is much good grass on the ranch for raising cattle. We use one or two for milk, even though, unlike Americans, milk is not such an important part of our Filipino diet, even for children. We freeze the milk to use until we get enough for all the kids. They do enjoy cups of milk and milk with oatmeal."

Larry and I have brought boxes of chocolate pudding, gummy worms, coconut, and green food color to make dirt dessert with the kids. When we first came to the ranch, the cooking was done on a propane range using big soup pots, and the ever-present, extra-large size electric rice cooker. Once in a while, a student will build a fire pit, ringed by rocks and cook something special, like corn on the cob, using the wood for fuel that is in such abundant supply, especially after a typhoon knocks down trees.

To save money on propane, Celing and his crew built a covered kitchen outside the dining hall with a large grill, heated by wood. This is one of the most recent renovations.

Lorraine, gorgeous, cool, and funniest Mommy chef says, "Oatmeal with milk? Oatmeal with cinnamon? Oatmeal with honey? Oatmeal with syrup? Come and get it with cocoa!" She laughed. "I rarely cook. Poppy was always the best cook at our house! So living here is the best: I always hire a cook! Hehehe!"

One night after Larry and I had just gone to bed, one of the kids came banging on our door, "Make sure your doors and windows are closed real tight! It's a typhoon!"

The wind howled! We heard crashing and cracking! The next day we enjoyed roasted fresh green banana and banana soup from the trees that had been ripped up by the roots.

"When a typhoon knocks our trees down, we cut them into firewood and use it for our outdoor kitchen, and sell what we can't use."

Fresh bananas are a treat, especially after a typhoon. The cooks prepare them in a variety of ways for several meals, so none go to waste.

The morning, after the typhoon, the kids worked in teams to drag broken trees to the area where Celing and older boys chopped them into firewood.
God gives wisdom to turn potential tragedies into triumphs!

We ate in the dining room with the kids every day.

Typical breakfasts on the ranch are rice, noodles, or oatmeal,
served with little cookies from the bakery.

The cooks prepare Jackfruit, which grows attached to the trunk of a tree
on the ranch. The jackfruit grows to about 36 inches long and is delicious in
soups. Jasmine (her chosen pseudonym) helps pick a jackfruit on the ranch.

Most lunches and dinners

Taro root grows all over the world in warm climates. It tastes much like potatoes. The
root can be roasted, boiled, and fried. It can be ground and used as flour and made
into pancakes. The leaves and stems can also be cooked. Many poor people who
live in the countryside away from the cities use taro as a main part of their diet. Taro
grows in the garden on the ranch. It is delicious in soups.

Calamansi, a sour green fruit, the size of a grape, is delicious, especially squeezed over fish. Calamansi grows on trees behind the girls' and boys' houses. Lorraine and Celing planted them several years ago. Sometimes calamansi is mixed with soy sauce.

Almost every meal in the Philippines contains the staple food, rice. Rice for lunches and dinners is often accompanied by soup made from a variety of vegetables either from the market or from the garden and rice with chicken. The cook chops chickens, complete with bones and boiled with vegetables to make soup. The bones provide calcium. The children put saucers on each table for the bones, which are then thrown outside for the small ranch animals.

Lorraine buys forty or fifty chickens at a time from two different markets in Lucena City. Quite often, vendors ride their bicycles or motor bikes to the ranch with a variety of fish. Celing is the best judge if the fish are fresh or not, since from his childhood, he was a fisherman. The most common fish is tilapia. But as a treat, we had minnows, which are salted and deep fried until they are crispy, heads, tails, bones, and all. (Becky, our granddaughter and I enjoyed them, like popcorn. Larry couldn't face the beady little eyeballs!) Other kinds of fish are gutted, then fried or boiled, complete with heads and tails.

The children watched us closely to see how we dealt with the heads. Then they all laughed at our squeamish reactions. We laughed, too, making it a fun time.

Most recently, Celing and his crew have completed ponds on the ranch to raise tilapia. They have been harvesting fresh tilapia of 12-14 inches. Now that's fresh!

When Lorraine's mom and dad, Kay and Mario DiGesu (Nanny and Poppy) come to the ranch they always send pinto beans ahead. Poppy, an accomplished chef, cooks up a big pot of beans, and quite often he makes the left-overs into chili. The children aren't too fond of the chili, since spicy food is not their normal fare.

Poppy, Lorraine's dad, loves cooking for the kids. Beans and chili are his specialties. We spent some time with both Nanny and Poppy on the ranch.

Once or twice a year, Celing buys a pig from a neighbor. They kill it, clean it, chop it into selected meat parts, and freeze sections. A special treat for Filipinos is pig blood soup, but visitors like us, rarely try it.

Adobo is the favorite Filipino food. Adobo is made with chunks of chicken or beef and potatoes, very much like American stew. Pancit is another favorite made with rice noodles, chicken, and vegetables. Lorraine introduced us to the most amazing dessert: halo-halo. It is made with purple yam ice cream, coconut ice cream, white beans, fruit and ice. Mmmm, our favorite.

17 LIMITLESS DEDICATION

Psalm 63:1 KJV O God, thou art my God; early will I seek thee: my soul thirsteth for thee, my flesh longeth for thee in a dry and thirsty land.

How does one deal with a child who runs away…away from safety…away from those who have committed themselves to safety and well-being?

Lorraine and Celing deal with each child individually, just as God deals with each of us.

Milo (his chosen fictitious name) came to the ranch from DSWD at a young age. He was a feisty little boy. It took him a long time to bond with Mommy and Daddy and even longer to accept the rules and responsibilities. Despite the fact that he received three meals a day and clean clothes and a safe place to sleep, the strong little four-year old decided to run away from the ranch.

"I hate you!" Milo yelled. Crying and screaming, he ran down the driveway and away from the ranch. He made it all the way down the lane to the little village just outside the ranch before Celing caught up with him.

Milo had no idea where he was going, or how he would eat, or where he would sleep. He just ran…away from safety…away from love.

"It's time to come home," Celing said in Tagalog, in a kind voice. He bent down to the little boy's level.

"Noooo!" little Milo yelled. He hit Celing with his fists.

In one swift move, Celing scooped the little boy up over his shoulder.

"Nooo!" wailed the little boy. He struggled against Celing's grip. Milo pulled Celing's hair, kicked with his bare feet, and hit Celing's strong back with his fists, all the time screaming at the top of his lungs!

Celing held onto the struggling little boy, until Milo chomped down on his back. Even though Milo still had his baby teeth, the sudden pinch caused Celing to swiftly lower the little boy to the ground.

"Owee!" Celing yelled.

Milo scrambled up and started running again.

The thought flashed through Celing's mind, "Should I just let him go?"

But the next thought had to be from the Lord's Holy Spirit, "I have chosen Milo for you to make a difference in his life."

Once again, Celing grabbed up the little boy. This time, he put him in a 'fireman's carry, so Milo couldn't kick and hit. The little boy finally quit fighting.

Celing made his way up the sloping road lined with palm trees, thorn bushes, and vines, attempting to trip his progress back home. When he finally reached the entry-way, Celing squatted down and cradled the now-quiet, little boy, like he would a precious baby.

Their eyes met. Milo's eyes were red from crying. His short black hair stuck flat to his head.

"What do you want to do?" Celing asked the little boy.

"Go home, Daddy," Milo said as silent tears slid down his cheeks.

"Will you walk with me?" Celing asked. They stood up. The man held out his hand to the little boy.

"Yes, Daddy." Milo took Daddy's hand. They walked to the house together.

Lorraine met them at the door.

"I'm sorry, Mommy," Milo said, looking down at the floor.

She knelt down by the little boy and whispered in his ear.

Milo looked at Lorraine and nodded his head.

She whispered again. Milo left the house. A few minutes later he came back with his blanket. Lorraine helped him make a bed on the floor.

"Good night, Mommy," Milo said, sleepily. He rolled over and fell asleep immediately.

"Daddy, that little blessing is exactly why the Lord has us here." Lorraine put her hand on her husband's back.

"Ow! That 'little blessing' bit me right there!"

Now Milo is a hard worker and the joy of the Lord
and limitless dedication shine in his life.

18   COUNT YOUR BLESSINGS

John 14:23 KJV Jesus answered and said unto him, If a man love me, he will keep my words: and my Father will love him, and we will come unto him, and make our abode with him.

Psalm 28:7 The LORD is my strength and my shield; my heart trusted in him, and I am helped: therefore my heart greatly rejoiceth; and with my song will I praise him.

Children come to FHL from many different avenues. Four little boys, each about the age of three, were picked up together. It was determined that the parents had sold them for drugs. The little boys were too young to know anything of their own personal history so they were given the same last name, which was the name of the street where they were picked up. The name was a convenient identifier. Because a birth certificate is required to process children into the government system, the boys, who are not related, were given the same birth date. When Lorraine was able to bring the boys to the ranch, she allowed them to choose new first names, since the only names they knew were not reflective of the potential for each of the boys. At first they were glad for the safety, reliable three meals every day, and the security of the ranch. As days stretched into months, and months into years, the four boys developed vastly different personalities.

When Larry and I first met the boys, they knew only a few words of English. We both helped them with new English words by drawing pictures and getting older students to translate for us. Carlo, Jared, and Jim began to excel in school. When we came to the ranch two years later, three of the four boys remembered us and were happy to see us. They were speaking such excellent English, that they loved talking to us and showing us all the new things on the ranch.

Only Norton seemed shy and wouldn't talk to us. One evening, one of the care-givers told Norton to take his clothes off the line and take his bath.

"No!" he cried in a loud voice. Carlo and Jared tried to get Norton to obey. They grabbed him by the arms, but he wrenched free and ran to the far side of the boys' dorm. He sank down like a wounded chicken. No one followed him so he sat there alone and big angry tears slid down his cheeks.

Carlo ran to tell Mommy what had happened.

The Philippine Islands are so close to the equator, that when the sun sets, darkness immediately drops like a big black curtain in a play.

Lorraine usually waits for an upset child to gather their composure, but in cases like Norton, the Holy Spirit let her know that it was important to let Norton know, she would not allow him to walk away alone in the darkness.

Lorraine had been sweeping their house in her bare feet. She dropped the bamboo broom. When she got to the water pump where the boys were bathing, they all pointed in the direction Norton had gone.

There she found him, crouched down, with his head on his knees, crying loudly. Lorraine sat crouched down beside him without saying a word.

"Go away!" Norton yelled, without looking at her.

She didn't say a word.

Norton got up and walked toward the edge of the property where the tall grass had not been mowed. He was still crying, sobbing, yelling incoherently.

"I'm going…away!" Norton's eyes squinted as he gazed into the dark.

"You know spiders live in tall grass…some spiders are poisonous," Mommy whispered. "Snakes… big boa constrictors and…and… deadly cobras live in tall grass."

"I don't care! Nobody cares. I hate everybody!" Norton yelled, and took one step into the grass.

"I'm coming with you," Lorraine said.

Norton felt the tall grass against his legs. There was no moon so it was really, really dark.

"Stop crying and count to twenty," Mommy said, quietly.

"No!" He yelled, and forced himself to cry louder.

Mommy waited.

He had to stop long enough to take a big breath.

"Stop crying and count to thirty," Mommy said.

"No!"

"You wait right here," Lorraine said. With long strides, she went to the hut and grabbed a bamboo mat. She was gone no more than four minutes, but to the little boy, alone in the dark, in the tall grass, hearing rustlings, it must have seemed like forever.

"Now we can have something to sleep on," she said simply, when she returned with the bamboo mat tucked under her arm.

"Are you running away, too, Mommy?" Norton asked, surprised.

"Yup!" she said. "If you go, I go, too. Unless, of course, you are ready to count to forty, and quit crying."

She took a high step, into the tall grass that came over her knees.

The grass reached above Norton's waist.

"Lord, I'm counting on You to keep the snakes and spiders away," she prayed silently.

Step by step, Mommy and the little boy walked toward the rushing sound of the creek.

"Do you think this is far enough for our first night?" Lorraine asked.

"Yes, Mommy."

Lorraine spread the mat on the ground. They sat down. The stars looked like a million tiny candles in the sky.

"Do you think God is up there, Mommy?" Norton asked.

"Yes, I know God is everywhere, Norton," she replied.

"Is God so far away?" he asked.

"No, Norton. God is right here." She put her hand on his heart. She could feel his heart beating in his skinny chest.

"Oh," was all he could think of to say.

They were quiet for a long time.

"Can we go home now?" the little boy asked.

"How can we go home? We're running away," she said simply.

"Oh, yeah," he said.

They were quiet for a long time. A falling star streaked across the dark sky.

"Did you see that, Mommy?" he asked.

"Yes. Poppy always told me when you see a falling star, someone just died." Mommy added.

"Oh," he said. He rubbed his eyes and leaned against Mommy. "Do you think it might be somebody we know?"

"I hope not," she said, quietly.

"Do you think God is mad at us because we're running away?" he asked.

"I know it makes God sad, because it's like we don't care about the rest of the kids on the ranch," Mommy said.

"Do you care about them, Mommy?" he asked.

"Norton, you know I love all the kids. And I love you, or I wouldn't be out here in the tall grass with snakes and spiders and…" She tickled his ribs.

Norton giggled.

"I'm ready to count to forty. Then, can we go back home, now?" he asked, standing up. He took Mommy's hand and pulled her up.

"What about running away?" she asked.

"Maybe running away is a bad idea," he said. He pulled her hand.

"Don't you think we should take our sleeping mat, just in case?" she asked.

"Yes," he said. He bent over and rolled the mat up and put it on his shoulder.

"One, two, three, four, five, six…" Hand-in-hand, they walked back through the tall grass to the house. It was late. All the boys were asleep already in the boys' house.

"You come sleep on our floor on the sleeping mat, so we don't disturb the others," Mommy said.

"Yes, Mommy. Thank you," he said.

They opened the screen door.

"Good night," Mommy said.

"Good night, Mommy," Norton said.

Lorraine stood by the screen door listening to all the sounds of the ranch. She heard the turkeys on the short wall saying their good nights. A night owl soared close to the house in search of a mouse. She smiled to herself as soft sounds of snoring came from the boys' house. Far in the background was the sound of the stream rushing its way over the rocks to the sea, only a few miles down the hill.

"Dear Lord," she breathed, "thank you for all these children, even when we are afraid. Continue giving me wisdom, so I will be ready for tomorrow's challenges." She smiled at the starry sky. "And thank You, Lord, we didn't meet a big snake or a poisonous spider. Good night, Lord Jesus."

19   MERCY UNBRIDLED X7

Psalm 13:5 KJV But I have trusted in thy mercy; my heart shall rejoice in thy salvation.

Despite the fact that the children come to live in a safe, loving, disciplined, godly environment, sometimes their past continues to haunt them. Satan loves to stir up the memories of their own bad choices, accusing them to the point where they wish for self-destruction.

How does Mommy Lorraine, the Kid Whisperer, confront such evil?

Psalm 46:1 KJV God is our refuge and strength, a very present help in trouble.

Lorraine explains it this way: "In my own life, the only time I thought of it (suicide) was when mom and dad were fighting and my siblings and I would talk about 'what if?' What if, mom and dad divorced? Which one will you choose to live with? My thoughts were neither of them. If they can't work it out and make it in this world, neither can I. So in my little mind, I thought if they divorce, I would consider suicide. Anyway, a few of my friends committed suicide when their parents divorced. So I thought that would be the cure from the pain."

"I had seriously given my life to Jesus at a young age. I know God saved my life and my parent's marriage. At that time, I made a deal with God: If my parents do not divorce, I will serve the Lord wherever He calls me. My dream then was to go to India to follow my idol, Mother Teresa, but God opened the door for me to go to the Philippines."

"Now we work with and live amongst broken children whose parents actually do separate or divorce. In the Philippines, annulment of a marriage is more common, but even that is impossible for poor people because annulment requires legal fees. The children who are left behind have plenty of reasons for wanting to end their lives. I know if I were in their shoes, I would have taken my life already. It's too much to bear for anyone, much less a little person. So we try our best to make the Ranch their secure home. Hug them in the morning and at night. Kiss them on the forehead to show them that they are loved. Play with them and chat about silly things. In the mornings, I lead the young ones in prayer and devotions before school starts. The older ones I have night devotions and prayer. These times are all very personal."

Lorraine told the story of one of their boys. "One of the first boys that came in 2004, was 3 years old. He lived with us until he was 9. Then he was reunited with his father, who had just gotten out of jail. During those five years of being with his family, he had no chance to go to school and lived in the 'squatter,' with no running water or proper sewage, and little food. He was pushed around by his older brothers to bring drugs back and forth. Later, he told me he had never thought of suicide at the ranch. Only when he went back to his real family did he think of taking his life. In 2014, he came back to us, asking for help. He was physically, mentally, and spiritually beat up and tired of living. He is now happily back at the ranch, in school, president of his class, great in sports and getting good grades."

"None of our children ever considered suicide before, not outside or inside the ranch... until I went to America for a short while. I continued to pray for the kids but somehow, Satan got ahold of them."

One of the FHL girls, Frannie (her chosen pseudonym) told me (the author) her story:

"I had just turned twelve. I had been at the ranch for two years. Mommy went to the United States. I started thinking about what an awful person I had been before I came to Mommy. I felt worse and worse, like I didn't deserve to live. Then Mommy came back. I finally went and cried and cried to Mommy and told her everything. After that, Mommy prayed for me and talked to me for a long time. Every day Mommy spent time with me just listening and talking. My life got better. I really wanted to end my life before, but then Mommy gave me hope and she said that in Christ Jesus, I can be changed and loved."

Frannie, clowning with her friends for my camera, had
earned the privilege of eating in the bamboo hut.

Frannie is now studying at Saint Augustine School of Nursing. Frannie went on to explain, "Jesus has been real to me because He changed my life and it has made a big difference to me. I believe that if I had not received Him I wouldn't be able to see His plan for me. In spite of our wrong choices, Mommy still loves us and cares for us. She is a blessing to me, because without her, I wouldn't be inspired to achieve my goals."

20   FORGIVENESS 7X70

Matthew 18:21-22 KJV
Then came Peter to Him and said,
"Lord, how often shall my brother sin against me, and I forgive him?
til seven times?"
Jesus saith unto him, "I say not unto thee, until seven times:
but until seventy times seven."

Zig Ziglar- Remember when you forgive, you heal.
And when you let go, you grow.

Anger is a typical reaction of children when they first come to the ranch. They are angry at their families, angry about being hungry, angry at all those who used and abused them. Many are even angry at God, even though they have never met Jesus.

Lorraine explained: "Anger management starts with self-management! Self-control and the other fruits of the Spirit (Galatians 5:22-23) come into play at this moment. I say a quick prayer for wisdom before I act. Every situation is different because every child is different. There is no formula or quick fix to dealing with their anger. They have a reason to be angry. They have been neglected, abused, and rejected. Anything can trigger them. Even though they are in a safe and loving environment, the pain is still there and lots of trust issues. And why should they trust anyone? Their very own flesh and blood hurt them and turned on them."

"Running is a good way to release anger. They run laps around the court or dining hall to match their age. Doing extra chores, puts their anger-generated energy to good use!"

"Sometimes, just a big hug to squeeze the anger out of them works. Heheh."

"Sometimes when they are angry, they won't talk to us, so we leave them alone for a little while to think about it and sort things out in their mind. They have notebooks to write things down if they can't talk about it."

"The best solution is to talk and pray with them and reassure them that it's ok to be angry sometimes but we must deal with it as it comes so it doesn't affect their future."

"Jesus got angry too, but for a cause with a purpose. We have to make sure our anger does the same. The Lord can make beauty from ashes."

Isaiah 61:3 KJV
To appoint unto them that mourn in Zion,
To give unto them beauty for ashes,
The oil of joy for mourning,
The garment of praise for the spirit of heaviness;
That they might be called trees of righteousness,
The planting of the LORD, THAT HE MIGHT BE glorified.

Showing mercy and compassion for others plays a huge part in building any organization that reaches out to lost souls. DJ shared with us how they felt when they went to pick up the first two boys chosen to come to FHL.

Running, with or without a kite, discipline, hugs, and lots of love make once sad, rejected children into joyful kiddos. Trust and real joy goes two ways, as shown by the kids with Larry, the author's husband.

The author and her husband enjoy a view of volcanoes, the building blocks of the Philippine Islands. More than 7,000 volcanoes have pushed up from the ocean floor of the Pacific Ocean to form islands and atolls.

"The boys have several siblings, but the oldest we could take could only be 10 years old. The older brother had helped his two younger brothers get ready to go. Perhaps he had given them the best they had in their dwelling. It was raining. Micah and I sat in the van watching. The older brother hugged the two younger boys, with rain dripping off his long hair. Tears stung his eyes. He stood watching as his two brothers climbed into the van."

The conversation may have gone something like this:

"Mommy, he's crying," Micah said, shaking her shoulder.

Mommy Lorraine looked at the lone boy standing alone, with no umbrella.

"Daddy, can't we take him, too?" DJ asked. "He is old enough to help with his brothers!"

Daddy Celing asked Lorraine, "That makes sense, Lorraine. We could take him and do the paper-work when we get home."

"We need to do it right, Daddy," Lorraine said with tears in her own eyes.

One hour later they were back with all the papers and the older brother joined his brothers at the ranch.

The whole experience motivated DJ to write one of his first songs.

DESPERATE FOR LOVE
By Dave Lamar
I stood there in the silence staring at this boy.
I could see the anger in his eyes and he was ready to destroy.
His heart was full of hatred for what he went through in the past.
And even at that moment he was feeling so out cast.

CODA
He's crying out in the rain
So no one could see his pain.

CHORUS
Because he's desperate for love,
He needs some help from above
And he is crying out in fear,
He needs someone to wipe away his tears.
He knows his heart is broken,
He needs the Healer to come restore him,
All he wants is peace in his heart,
He should have been loved right from the start.
But it seems his mother's always shouting,
And his dad is never home.
He always takes the beating when she gets out of control.
He's hungry and exhausted from working all day long,
Because he takes care of his sister,
And he has to feed her on his own.

BRIDGE
He should have been loved right from the start,
He never deserved this broken heart,
He never deserved this kind of life he's going through.
He needs to feel this loving touch,
And someone to say, "I love you so much,"
Because he's never heard those words.

21 ADAPTING TO GOD'S NEW PLAN

Isaiah 49:13 KJV Sing, O heavens; and be joyful, O earth; and
break forth into singing, O mountains: for the LORD hath comforted
his people, and will have mercy upon his afflicted.

New beginnings are not easy. Mommy Lorraine and Daddy Celings's idea was to take children between the ages of 3 up to age 10. The plan was to raise each one as their own child and help them transition into a successful, hopeful life as a responsible adult. The new rules of the government treated all orphanages the same and made the 6 month rule: Children must either be adopted by a family or returned to their original family after 6 months, or no longer than 1 year.

But God is always in charge whether we or the government likes it or not.

Mommy Lorraine and Daddy Celing adopted three of the children themselves. Now, Mommy and Daddy are adapting to the new plan. Lorraine expressed her renewed joy for the Lord's new plan this way:

"Our first baby was adopted by a family in Spain after we cared for him for a year. Our second baby will be adopted by a family in France at the end of this year. Four siblings were adopted by a great Christian family. One of our older boys was finally united with his brother in Canada."

"It was our first year to stop homeschooling our high school kids. We have sent them to the public school and what a light and example they have been, to many other students and their teachers. The ranch is their hang-out place when they don't have class. And we have a Bible study for them."

"The kids that had already been with us for several years were sent back to their families, where they had been neglected in their young years. Many of them took bad turns in life. The adoption route is much better."

Psalm 37:4-6 KJV Delight thyself also in the LORD; and
he shall give thee the desires of thine heart.

Commit thy way unto the LORD; trust also in him; and he shall bring it to pass.
And he shall bring forth thy righteousness as the light,
and thy judgment as the noonday.

"It is important to understand that the key to God giving us the desires of our heart is in committing our lives to Him. As we truly surrender our life to God, His desires begin to become our desires. His desire is to save the lost and heal the broken-hearted. God has a plan and purpose for our lives. If we are committed to following His plan, then He will only give to us what He has planned for us."

22   WE DESIRE TO BE A BLESSING NOT A BURDEN

1Samuel 2:8 KJV He raiseth up the poor out of the dust, and lifteth up the beggar from the dunghill, to set them among princes, and to make them inherit the throne of glory: for the pillars of the earth are the LORD'S...

Lorraine explains her driving desire:

"It is my desire that these children can enjoy the benefits of being a blessing and not a burden to society. Surrendering our lives to God is the goal!"

"Ask yourself what is in your heart? Do you really desire to live a life dedicated to God? If so, then surrendering your will to Him and asking for help will come naturally."

"Once I tasted of the amazing love that He gives and began to experience His presence in my life, I began to yearn for more of all that He could be in my life. When I notice the key verbs in Psalm 119:33-37 (paraphrased): Teach me, oh Lord, Your laws… Give me understanding…Direct my heart in Your paths…Turn my heart towards You and not toward selfish gain…Turn my eyes away from myself, and preserve my life according to Your Word!

I pay attention to the verbs:

<u>Teach</u> me.

<u>Give</u> me understanding.

<u>Direct</u> me.

<u>Turn</u> my heart.

<u>Turn</u> my eyes.

"All we have to do is trust our Lord Jesus to make the changes in our lives, then follow as He directs us with His Holy Spirit."

"Recently I had a reason to really get upset about something. An organization that I had been leading in Sunday morning worship planned a special event. Instead of asking me to lead worship, they brought in someone from another place. I wrestled with my pride. Then I remembered how God works. In order to be 'a somebody' in God's Kingdom, you must become 'a nobody' first."

"Then the Lord reminded me in His Word:

Matthew 5:3 KJV Blessed are the poor in spirit,
for theirs is the kingdom of Heaven.

"As I got a grip on my spiritual self, I decided to let the situation go, and become a team player rather than a complainer. And that is when the peace of the Holy Spirit came upon me! Maintaining a humble attitude, in the midst of trials, like this one, and allowing the Lord to be glorified in every situation, is the key to being somebody in the Kingdom of Heaven on Earth. Is there anything more important than that?"

Typical breakfasts on the ranch are rice, noodles, or oatmeal, served with little cookies from the bakery.

"As I got a grip on my spiritual self, I decided to let the situation go, and become a team player rather than a complainer. And that is when the peace of the Holy Spirit came upon me! Maintaining a humble attitude, in the midst of trials, like this one, and allowing the Lord to be glorified in every situation, is the key to being somebody in the Kingdom of Heaven on Earth. Is there anything more important than that?"

Each new day at FAITH, HOPE, & LOVE Kids Ranch brings new challenges as well as new blessings. For recipes and definitions visit: ruthsbooks.com For more about FAITH, HOPE, & LOVE Kids Ranch visit Lorraine DiGesu Lamar on Facebook.

CPSIA information can be obtained
at www.ICGtesting.com
Printed in the USA
LVHW072308231218
600810LV00011B/9/P